AF457353

NCERT
QUESTION-ANSWERS
ENGLISH
Language & Literature

ENGLISH

Language & Literature

CLASS 9th

by
Kapil Sabharwal

ARIHANT PRAKASHAN, MEERUT

ARIHANT PRAKASHAN, MEERUT

Administrative & Production Offices

Corporate Office: 'Ramchhaya' 4577/15, Agarwal Road, Darya Ganj, New Delhi -110002
Tele: 011- 47630600, 43518550; Fax: 011- 23280316

Head Office: Kalindi, TP Nagar, Meerut (UP) - 250002
Tele: 0121-2401479, 2512970, 4004199; Fax: 0121-2401648

All disputes subject to Meerut (UP) jurisdiction only.

Sales & Support Offices

Agra, Ahmedabad, Bengaluru, Bhubaneswar, Bareilly, Chennai, Delhi, Guwahati, Haldwani
Hyderabad, Jaipur, Jalandhar, Jhansi, Kolkata, Kota, Lucknow, Meerut, Nagpur & Pune

ISBN 978-93-5141-465-0

Typeset by Arihant DTP Unit at Meerut

For further information about the products from Arihant
log on to **www.arihantbooks.com** or email to **info@arihantbooks.com**

Preface

Feeling the immense importance and value of NCERT books, we are presenting this book, having the NCERT Exercises Solutions. For the overall benefit of the students we have made this book unique in such a way that it presents not only solutions but also detailed explanations. Through these detailed and through explanations, students can learn the concepts which will enhance their thinking and learning abilities.

Explanatory Solutions have been provided to all the questions given in each chapter of NCERT book. We have given all the points that tell how to approach to solve a problem. Here we have tried to cover all those loopholes which may lead to confusion. All formulae and hints are discussed in full detail.

Apart from all those who helped in the compilation of this book a special note of thanks to Ms Karishma Yadav (Project Head) and Ms Aleena Zaidi (Project Coordinator). With the hope that this book will be of great help to the students, I wish great success to my readers.

Kapil Sabharwal

Contents

Term I

Prose 3-52

Poetry 53-67

Supplementary Reader 68-87

Term II

Prose 91-129

Poetry 130-141

Supplementary Reader 142-158

Term I

Prose

1

The Fun They Had

Issac Asimov

Chapter Sketch

'The Fun They Had' written by Isaac Asimov is set in the future. Through the story, the writer tries to see a future where books and schools as we know them today will perhaps not exist. According to the writer, the students of that time will not be able to have fun like we do.

Detailed Summary

Margie Writes about a 'Real' Book

Margie wrote on 17 May, 2157, in her diary that Tommy found a real book! The book was very old. Margie's grandfather once told her that when he was a child, his grandfather told him that there was a time when all stories were printed on paper.

The pages were yellow and crinkly. The words didn't move like they did on the screen. It was a whole new experience. Tommy thought it was a waste as their television screen had a million books on it. Margie enquired about the book. Tommy told her that he found it in the attic and it was about school.

Margie Hates School

Margie went scornful. She hated school. She always hated school but now, she hated it more than ever. The 'mechanical' teacher had been giving her test after test in Geography and she had been doing worse and worse. Finally, her mother sent for the County Inspector.

The County Inspector was a round little man with a red face. He took the teacher apart. Margie had hoped he wouldn't know how to put it together again, but he did it.

The Mechanical Learning

The mechanical teacher was large, black and ugly. It had a big screen on which all the lessons were shown and the questions were asked. The part Margie hated most was the slot where she had to put homework and test papers. She had to write them in a punch code which she had learned when she was six. The inspector told her mother that the poor score was not Margie's fault. The Geography sector was geared a little too quick, but he set it right to an average ten year level. He was satisfied with Margie's overall progress.

Tommy Tells Margie about Old Schools

Margie hated school so much that she hoped that they would take her mechanical teacher away. They took Tommy's away when its history sector blanked out. Margie wondered why would anyone write about school.

Tommy told her that it wasn't their kind of school. The book was about schools which existed centuries ago. Margie was hurt because she didn't know about them. She read the book and found that the schools had a teacher. Tommy informed her that it wasn't a regular teacher. It was a man. Margie was quite surprised to hear this.

The Old Schools

Tommy further told her that the teacher taught the boys and girls and gave them homework. Margie was skeptical about a man being smart enough. But Tommy said he was so. Margie said that she wouldn't want a strange man in her house. Tommy started laughing. He told her that the teacher didn't live in the house. There was a special building and all the kids went there. All the kids of the same age learned the same thing. Margie said that according to her mother a teacher has to be adjusted to fit the mind of each boy and girl it teaches. Each kid has to be taught differently. Tommy told her that it was the same thing, but was done differently.

The Fun They Had

They weren't even half way through the book when Margie's mother called her out. It was time for school. She asked Tommy, if she could read the book again. Tommy replied nonchalantly and went away tucking the book under his arm.

Margie went into the school room which was next to her bedroom. She had regular classes on the same time except for Saturday and Sunday as Mrs Jones believed that little girls learned better, if they studied at regular hours. Margie inserted her homework with a sigh. She was thinking about the old schools. She was thinking about the fun they had.

Exercises

Thinking about the Text

I. *Answer these questions in a few words or a couple of sentences each.*

Q 1. How old are Margie and Tommy?

Ans. Margie is eleven and Tommy is thirteen years old.

Q 2. What did Margie write in her diary?

Ans. Margie wrote in her diary,"Today Tommy found a real book!"

Q 3. Had Margie ever seen a book before?

Ans. No, Margie had never seen a book before.

Q 4. What things about the book did she find strange?

Ans. She found many things about the book which were strange to her. The pages were yellow and crinkly. The words didn't 'move'. When they turned back to the page before, it had the same words on it that had when they read it earlier.

Q 5. What do you think a telebook is?

Ans. A telebook is a virtual book that can be read on a screen. You don't have to turn pages, the words themselves move across the screen.

Q 6. Where was Margie's school? Did she have any classmates?

Ans. Margie's school was a room right next to her bedroom. No, she didn't have any classmates. Even her teacher was a machine.

Q 7. What subjects did Margie and Tommy learn?

Ans. They learnt History, Geography and Mathematics.

II. *Answer the following with reference to the story.*

Q 1. "I wouldn't throw *it* away".

(*i*) Who says these words?

(*ii*) What does 'it' refer to ?

(*iii*) What is it being compared with by the speaker?

Ans. (*i*) These words were said by Margie.

(*ii*) 'It' refers to the book.

(*iii*) The book is being compared with the virtual book.

Q 2. "Sure *they* had a teacher, but it wasn't a *regular* teacher. It was a man."

(*i*) Who does 'they' refer to?

(*ii*) What does 'regular' mean here?

(*iii*) What is it contrasted with?

Ans. (*i*) 'They' refers to Tommy's grandfather's forefathers.

(*ii*) It means 'of the usual kind.'

(*iii*) It is being contrasted with a mechanical teacher.

III. *Answer each of these questions in a short paragraph (about 30 words).*

Q 1. What kind of teachers did Margie and Tommy have?

Ans. Margie and Tommy had a mechanical teacher. The robot-looking teacher had a big black screen on which all the lessons were shown and the questions were asked. The 'teacher' also had a slot where they had to put homework and test papers.

Q 2. Why did Margie's mother send for the County Inspector?

Ans. Margie's mother sent for the County Inspector because the mechanical teacher had been giving Margie test after test in Geography and she had been doing worse and worse. Her mother probably suspected that there was something wrong with the mechanical teacher.

Q 3. What did he do?

Ans. The County Inspector smiled at Margie and gave her an apple. Then he took the mechanical teacher apart. Margie had hoped that he wouldn't be able to put it back together, but he did.

Q 4. Why was Margie doing badly in Geography? What did the County Inspector do to help her?

Ans. As the Geography sector of the mechanical teacher was somehow adjusted to a higher level, Margie was performing poorly. It was above her level. The County Inspector slowed it up to an average ten year level, to help her.

Q 5. What had once happened to Tommy's teacher?

Ans. Tommy's teacher was taken away once for nearly a month because the history sector of the mechanical teacher had blanked out completely. Margie hoped the same for her mechanical teacher.

Q 6. Did Margie have regular days and hours for school? If so, why?

Ans. Yes, Margie certainly had regular days and hours for school. Margie had to attend her school at the same time everyday except for Saturday and Sunday. Her mother ensured this because according to her little girls learned better, if they learned at regular hours.

Q 7. How does Tommy describe the old kind of school?

Ans. Tommy said that the old kind of school existed centuries ago. Instead of a mechanical teacher, the teacher used to be a 'man'. All the students went to a special building where they all learned the same thing according to their respective ages.

Q 8. How does he describe the old kind of teachers?

Ans. Tommy said that the old kind of teacher was a 'man' who taught in a special building where all the kids went together. He told the kids things, gave them homework and asked questions.

IV. *Answer each of these questions in two or three paragraphs (100-150 words).*

Q 1. What are the main features of the mechanical teachers and the school rooms that Margie and Tommy have in the story?

Ans. Margie and Tommy have mechanical teachers. It means that they are not human, instead they are kind of robots. They have large black screens on which lessons are shown and questions are asked. The mechanical teachers also have mechanical voices. The students have to write their homework and test papers in a punch code and put it in a special slot after which the teacher calculates the marks. Each teacher is adjusted to the mind of its student.

They don't have schools or classmates. Margie's school room is a room right next to her bedroom. The mechanical teacher probably lives in her house. She gets lessons from it everyday at a specific time except for Saturdays and Sundays.

Q 2. Why did Margie hate school? Why did she think the old kind of school must have been fun?

Ans. The school to which Margie went to was a room right next to her bedroom. It wasn't fun at all. She had no classmates whatsoever and her teacher was a robot. Lately she had started to hate her school more as her mechanical teacher had been giving her test after test in Geography and she had been doing worse and worse. She hated it so much that she hoped that the County Inspector wouldn't be able to put her teacher back together.

She thought that the old schools must have been fun because there all the kids from the whole neighbourhood came, laughing and shouting in the school yard, sitting together in the school room and going home together at the end of the day. They learned the same things, so they could help one another with the homework and talk about it. Moreover, the teachers were people.

Q 3. Do you agree with Margie that schools today are more fun than the school in the story? Give reasons for your answer.

Ans. I totally agree with Margie that schools today are more fun than the school in the story. In the story, Margie has a school in her house! Her teacher is a robot and she has no classmates. One can imagine what a boring and dull school she was having. Whenever we hear the word school, images of children having all fun and frolic start running through our minds. This wasn't the case with Margie.

She couldn't play with her friends in the school playground or come home together with them nor she could think of helping one another with the homework. Moreover, the mechanical teachers gave test after test even if one wasn't performing well, without understanding the student's psyche.

Thinking about Language

I. *Adverbs*

Read this sentence taken from the story.

They had once taken Tommy's teacher away for nearly a month bacause the history sector had blanked out completely.

The word *complete* is an adjective. When you add –ly to it, it becomes an adverb.

Q 1. Find the sentences in the lesson which have the adverbs given in the box below

awfully	sorrowfully	completely	loftily
carefully	differently	quickly	nonchalantly

Ans. *The sentences in the lesson which have the adverbs are*

Awfully They turned the pages, which were yellow and crinkly and it was awfully funny to read words that stood still instead of moving the way they were supposed to – on a screen, you know.

Sorrowfully The mechanical teacher had been giving her test after test in Geography and she had been doing worse and worse until her mother had shaken her head sorrowfully and sent for County Inspector.

Completely They had once taken Tommy's teacher away for nearly a month because the history sector had blanked out completely.

Loftily and Carefully He added loftily, pronouncing the word carefully, "Centuries ago."

Differently But my mother says a teacher has to be adjusted to fit the mind of each boy and girl it teaches and that each kid has to be taught differently.

Quickly "I didn't say I didn't like it," Margie said quickly.

Nonchalantly "May be," he said nonchalantly.

Q 2. Now use these adverbs to fill in the blanks in the sentences below.

(*i*) The report must be read .... so that performance can be improved.

(*ii*) At the interview, Sameer answered our questions ...., shrugging his shoulders.

(*iii*) We all behave .... when we are tired or hungry.

(*iv*) The teacher shook her head .... when Ravi lied to her.

(*v*) I forgot about it ....

(*vi*) When I complimented Revathi on her success, she just smiled .... and turned away.

(*vii*) The president of the company is .... busy and will not be able to meet you.

(*viii*) I finished my work so that I could go out to play............ .

Ans. (*i*) carefully (*ii*) nonchalantly
(*iii*) differently (*iv*) sorrowfully
(*v*) completely (*vi*) loftily
(*vii*) awfully (*viii*) quickly

***Q* 3.** Make adverbs from these adjectives.

(*i*) Angry (*ii*) Happy
(*iii*) Merry (*iv*) Sleepy
(*v*) Easy (*vi*) Noisy
(*vii*) Tidy (*viii*) Gloomy

Ans. (*i*) Angry Angrily
(*ii*) Happy Happily
(*iii*) Merry Merrily
(*iv*) Sleepy Sleepily
(*v*) Easy Easily
(*vi*) Noisy Noisily
(*vii*) Tidy Tidily
(*viii*) Gloomy Gloomily

II. *Complete the following conditional sentences. Use the correct form of the verb.*

1. If I don't go to Anu's party tonight, ...
2. If you don't telephone the hotel to order food, ...
3. Unless you promise to write back, I ....
4. If she doesn't play any games, ...
5. Unless that little bird flies away quickly, the cat ....

Ans. 1. she will be angry.
2. you will miss your dinner.
3. will not talk to you.
4. she will become lazy.
5. will catch it.

Writing

Q. A new revised volume of Isaac Asimov's short stories has just been released. Order one set. Write a letter to the publisher, Mindfame Private Limited, 1632 Asaf Ali Road, New Delhi, requesting that a set be sent to you by Value Payable Post (VPP) and giving your address. *Your letter will have the following parts.*

Addresses of the sender and receiver

The salutation

The body of the letter

The closing phrases and signature

Ans. *E-1570*
RK Puram
New Delhi

April 4, 20XX

Mindframe Private Limited
1632, Asaf Ali Road
New Delhi

Dear Sir/Madam
I have come to know that you have just released a new revised volume of Isaac Asimov's short stories. I am a big fan of his writing style and the revised volume is really hard to find. Therefore, I would like to place an order for one set of the same. Kindly sent it to the above given address by Value Payable Post (VPP) after deducting the on going discount. Thanking you in advance.

Yours faithfully
Tushar

2

The Sound of Music

Deborah Cowley

Chapter Sketch

The two part chapter contains two stories. One is of Evelyn Glennie — a deaf girl who struggles with her handicap and finally becomes a world renowned musician. The next part is about Bismillah Khan — another renowned musician who conquered the world through his great music.

Part I

Detailed Summary

Evelyn Lost her Hearing at a Young Age

A seventeen years old Evelyn was going to the Royal Academy of Music in London. It was a daunting task for any budding musician. But it was more difficult for Evelyn as she was deaf. Evelyn Glennie's loss of hearing had been gradual. It was first noticed when she was eight. By eleven she was completely deaf due to nerve damage.

Evelyn doesn't Give up

She was determined to lead a normal life and pursue her interest in music. One day she noticed a girl playing a xylophone and decided that she wanted to play it too. Most of the teachers discouraged her but percussionist Ron Forbes spotted her potential. He began by tuning two large drums to different notes. Evelyn could feel the different notes of the drum in her body.

Never Looked Back After that

The rest was sheer determination and hardwork. She toured the United Kingdom with a youth orchestra and by the time she was sixteen, she had decided to make music her life. She auditioned for the Royal Academy of Music and scored one of the highest marks in the history of the academy. She gradually moved from orchestral work to solo performances. At the end of her three year course, she had captured most of the top awards.

How Evelyn Hears Music

She explains that music pours in through every part of her body. It tingles in the skin, her cheekbones and even in her hair. When she plays the xylophone, she can sense the sound passing up the stick into her fingertips. By leaning against the drums, she can feel the resonances flowing into her body. On a wooden platform she removes her shoes so that the vibrations pass through her bare feet and up her legs.

Evelyn—An Inspiration

She is a shining inspiration for deaf children. They see that there is nowhere that they cannot go. She has earned many awards and rewards. She has given enormous pleasure to millions.

Exercises

Thinking about the Text

I. *Answer these questions in a few words or a couple of sentences each.*

Q 1. How old was Evelyn when she went to the Royal Academy of Music?

Ans. Evelyn was about seventeen years old when she went to the Royal Academy of Music in London.

Q 2. When was her deafness first noticed? When was it confirmed?

Ans. Her deafness was first noticed by her mother when Evelyn was eight years old. Evelyn was waiting to play the piano. When her name was called, she did not move. Her mother suddenly realised that Evelyn had not heard anything.

Her deafness was confirmed when she was eleven. Her marks had deteriorated and her headmistress had urged her parents to take her to a specialist. They said that gradual nerve damage had severely impaired her hearing.

II. *Answer each of these questions in a short paragraph (30-40 words).*

Q 1. Who helped her to continue with music? What did he do and say?

Ans. Percussionist Ron Forbes was the first person who spotted Evelyn's potential. He began by tuning two large drums to different notes. He told Evelyn not to listen through her ears , but to try and sense the sound through some other way.

Suddenly Evelyn realised that she could feel the higher drum from the waist up and the lower drum from the waist down. Evelyn realised that she could sense certain notes in different parts of her body.

Q 2. Name the various places and causes for which Evelyn performs.

Ans. Evelyn has toured the United Kingdom with a youth orchestra. Apart from the regular concerts, she gives free concerts in prisons and hospitals. She gives high priority to classes for young musicians because of which she is a shining inspiration for deaf children.

III. *Answer the question in two or three paragraphs (100-150 words).*

Q 1. How does Evelyn hear music?

Ans. Evelyn is deaf. She cannot hear music like others. She hears music by sensing the notes in different parts of her body. Ron Forbes taught her to 'hear' like this. He tuned two drums to different notes and asked her to sense the sound in some other way. Evelyn realised that she could feel the higher drum from the waist up and the lower drum from the waist down.

When she plays the xylophone, she can sense the sound passing up the stick into her fingertips. By leaning against the drums, she can feel the resonances flowing into her body. On a wooden platform, she removes her shoes so that the vibrations could pass through her bare feet. She herself said that music poured in through every part of her body. It tingled in the skin, her cheekbones and even in her hair.

Part II

Pungi was Banned then Revived

Emperor Aurangzeb banned the playing of a musical instrument called *pungi* in the royal residence for it had a shrill unpleasant sound. A barber of a family of professional musicians decided to improve the tonal quality of the *pungi*. He chose a pipe with a natural hollow stem that was longer and broader than the *pungi* and made seven holes on the body of the pipe. When he played on it, closing and opening some of these holes, soft and melodious sounds were produced. He played the instrument before royalty and everyone was impressed. The instrument had to be given a new name. As the story goes, since it was first played in the Shah's chambers and was played by a *nai* (barber), the instrument was named the '*shehnai*'.

Ustad Bismillah Khan Brought *Shehnai* at the Front

The sound of the *shehnai* began to be considered auspicious. And for this reason it is still played in temples and is an indispensable component of any North Indian wedding. In the past, the *shehnai* was part of the *naubat* or traditional ensemble of nine instruments found at royal courts. The credit for bringing this instrument onto the classical stage goes to Ustad Bismillah Khan.

Music was in his Blood

Born on 21 March, 1916, Bismillah belongs to a well-known family of musicians from Bihar. His grandfather, Rasool Bux Khan, was the *shehnai-nawaz* of the Bhojpur king's court. His father, Paigambar Bux and other paternal ancestors were also great *shehnai* players.

At the age of three when his mother took him to his maternal uncle's house in Benaras (now Varanasi), Bismillah was fascinated watching his uncles practise the *shehnai*. He started accompanying uncle, Ali Bux, to the Vishnu temple of Benaras. Slowly, he started getting lessons in playing the instrument and would sit practicing throughout the day. For years to come the temple of Balaji and Mangala Maiya and the banks of the Ganga became the young apprentice's favourite haunts where he could practise in solitude. The flowing waters of the Ganga inspired him to improvise and invent ragas that were earlier considered to be beyond the range of the *shehnai*.

The Future was Bright

With the opening of the All India Radio in Lucknow in 1938 came Bismillah's big break. He soon became an often-heard *shehnai* player on radio. When India gained independence on 15 August, 1947, Bismillah Khan became the first Indian to greet the nation with his shehnai. His first trip abroad was to Afghanistan where King Zahir Shah was so taken in by the maestro that he gifted him priceless Persian carpets and other souvenirs. Film director Vijay Bhatt was so impressed after hearing him play at a festival that he named a film after the instrument called *Gunj Uthi Shehnai.*

A Renowned Musician

Bismillah Khan became the first Indian to be invited to perform at the prestigious Lincoln Centre Hall in the United States of America. National awards like the Padmashri, the Padma Bhushan and the Padma Vibhushan were conferred on him. In 2001,
Ustad Bismillah Khan was awarded India's highest civilian award, the Bharat Ratna.

A True Indian

Despite travelling many countries, he was exceedingly fond of Benaras and Dumraon and they remain for him the most wonderful towns of the world. He even denied a job in America saying that he cannot find the Ganga there. Whenever he was travelling abroad his heart kept aching for his homeland.

Exercises

Thinking about the Text

1. *Tick the right answer.*

Q 1. The (*shehnai, pungi*) was a 'reeded noisemaker.'

Ans. The *pungi* was a 'reeded noisemaker.'

Q 2. (Bismillah Khan, A barber, Ali Bux) transformed the *pungi* into a *shehnai*.

Ans. Ali Bux transformed the *pungi* into a *shehnai*.

Q 3. Bismillah Khan's paternal ancestors were (barbers, professional musicians).

Ans. Bismillah Khan's paternal ancestors were professional musicians.

Q 4. Bismillah Khan learnt to play the *shehnai* from (Ali Bux, Paigambar Bux, Ustad Faiyaaz Khan).

Ans. Bismillah Khan learnt to play the *shehnai* from his uncle Ali Bux.

Q 5. Bismillah Khan's first trip abroad was to (Afghanistan, USA, Canada).

Ans. Bismillah Khan's first trip abroad was to Afghanistan.

II. *Find the words in the text which show Ustad Bismillah Khan's feelings about the items listed below. Then mark a tick (✓) in the correct column. Discuss your answers in class.*

	Bismillah Khan's feelings about	Positive	Negative	Neutral
1.	Teaching children music			
2.	The film world			
3.	Migrating to the USA			
4.	Playing at temples			
5.	Getting the Bharat Ratna			
6.	The banks of the Ganga			
7.	Leaving Benaras and Dumraon			

Ans.

	Bismillah Khan's feelings about	Positive	Negative	Neutral
1.	Teaching children music	✓		
2.	The film world		✓	
3.	Migrating to the USA		✓	
4.	Playing at temples	✓		
5.	Getting the Bharat Ratna	✓		
6.	The banks of the Ganga	✓		
7.	Leaving Benaras and Dumraon		✓	

	Bismillah Khan's feelings about	Words in the text
1.	Teaching children music	With the coveted award resting on his chest and his eyes glinting with rare happiness he said, "All I would like to say is : Teach your children music, this is Hindustan's richest tradition; even the West is now coming to learn our music."
2.	The film world	"I just can't come to terms with the artificiality and glamour of the film world," he says with emphasis.
3.	Migrating to the USA	A student of his once wanted him to head a *shehnai* school in the USA and the student promised to recreate the atmosphere of Benaras by replicating the temples there. But Khansaab asked him if he would be able to transport River Ganga as well. Later he is remembered to have said, "That is why whenever I am in a foreign country, I keep yearning to see Hindustan."
4.	Playing at temples	Ustad Bismillah Khan's life is a perfect example of the rich, cultural heritage of India, one that effortlessly accepts that a devout Muslim like him can very naturally play the *shehnai* every morning at the Kashi Vishwanath temple.
5.	Getting the Bharat Ratna	With the coveted award resting on his chest and his eyes glinting with rare happiness he said, "All I would like to say is : Teach your children music, this is Hindustan's richest tradition; even the West is now coming to learn our music."
6.	The banks of the Ganga	The flowing waters of the Ganga inspired him to improvise and invent ragas that were earlier considered to be beyond the range of the *shehnai*.
7.	Leaving Benaras and Dumraon	Later he is remembered to have said, "That is why whenever I am in a foreign country, I keep yearning to see Hindustan. While in Mumbai, I think of only Benaras and the holy Ganga and while in Benaras, I miss the unique *mattha* of Dumraon."

III. *Answer these questions in 30–40 words.*

Q 1. Why did Aurangzeb ban the playing of the *pungi*?

Ans. Emperor Aurangzeb banned the playing of the *pungi* in the royal residence because it had a shrill and unpleasant sound. It became the generic name for reeded noisemakers.

Q 2. How is a *shehnai* different from a *pungi*?

Ans. Unlike *pungi, shehnai* is a pipe with a natural hollow stem that is longer and broader. It also has seven holes on its body. When it is played, the closing and opening of some of the holes produces soft and melodious sounds.

Q 3. Where was the *shehnai* played traditionally? How did Bismillah Khan change this?

Ans. *Shehnai* was part of the traditional ensemble of nine instruments found at royal courts collectively called as *naubat*. It was meant for auspicious occasions and was used only in temples and weddings.

Ustad Bismillah Khan brought in the change by bringing it onto the classical stage.

Q 4. When and how did Bismillah Khan get his big break?

Ans. Bismillah Khan had learned to play the *shehnai* from his uncle. He got his big break with the opening of the All India Radio in Lucknow in 1938. He soon became an often-heard *shehnai* player on radio.

Q 5. Where did Bismillah Khan play the *shehnai* on 15 August, 1947? Why was the event historic?

Ans. On 15 August, 1947, Bismillah Khan played the *shehnai* from the Red Fort. It was a historic day as India gained independence on that day. He became the first Indian to greet the nation with his *shehnai*.

Q 6. Why did Bismillah Khan refuse to start a *shehnai* school in the USA?

Ans. Bismillah Khan's student had once asked him to head a music school in the USA, but he refused because he could not live outside India. The student promised that he would recreate the atmosphere of Benaras by replicating the temples in the city. To this Bismillah Khan wanted to know if his student could also transport the River Ganga.

Q 7. Find at least two instances in the text which tell you that Bismillah Khan loves India and Benaras.

Ans. Bismillah Khan immensely loved India, particularly Benaras and Dumraon. The temple of Balaji, Mangala Maiya and the banks of River Ganga in Benaras were his favourite haunts. River Ganga's flowing waters inspired him to improvise and invent ragas that were once thought to be beyond the range of *shehnai*.

Bismillah Khan refused to start a *shehnai* school in the USA because he could not live outside India. When he was abroad his heart kept aching to return back to Hindustan.

Thinking about Language

I. *Complete the following sentences. Beginning with a to-verb, try to answer the questions in brackets.*

1. The school sports team hopes .... (What does it hope to do?)
2. We all want .... (What do we all want to do?)
3. They advised the hearing-impaired child's mother .... (What did they advise her to do?)
4. The authorities permitted us to .... (What did the authorities permit us to do?)
5. A musician decided to .... (What did the musician decide to do?)

Ans.
1. The school sports team hopes to win the tournament.
2. We all want to succeed.
3. They advised the hearing-impaired child's mother to take special care of her.
4. The authorities permitted us to play.
5. A musician decided to play a new raaga.

II. *From the text on Bismillah Khan, find the words and phrases that match these definitions and write them down. The number of the paragraph where you will find the words/phrases has been given for you in brackets.*

1. the home of royal people (1) ....
2. the state of being alone (5) ....
3. a part which is absolutely necessary (2) ....

4. to do something not done before (5) ....
5. without much effort (13) ....
6. quickly and in large quantities (9) .... and ....

Ans.
1. The home of royal people (1) the royal residence
2. The state of being alone (5) solitude
3. A part which is absolutely necessary (2) an indispensable component
4. To do something not done before (5) improvise
5. Without much effort (13) effortlessly
6. Quickly and in large quantities (9) thick and fast

III. *Tick the right answer.*

1. When something is revived, it (remains dead/lives again).
2. When a government bans something, it wants it (stopped/started).
3. When something is considered auspicious, (welcome it/avoid it).
4. When we take to something, we find it (boring/interesting).
5. When you appreciate something, you (find it good and useful/find it of no use).
6. When you replicate something, you do it (for the first time/for the second time).
7. When we come to terms with something, it is (still upsetting/no longer upsetting).

Ans.
1. When something is revived, it lives again.
2. When a government bans something, it wants it stopped.
3. When something is considered auspicious, welcome it.
4. When we take to something, we find it interesting.
5. When you appreciate something, you find it good and useful.
6. When you replicate something, you do it for the second time.
7. When we come to terms with something, it is no longer upsetting.

3

The Little Girl

Katherine Mansfield

Chapter Sketch

This story is about a little girl whose feelings for her father change from fear to understanding. At first her father is a figure she is scared of. But eventually things change and she creates a liking for her father.

Detailed Summary

Kezia is Scared of her Father

Kezia was apparently scared of her father. She would be glad when he left the house for work. In the evening Kezia would take off his shoes. She stammered in front of him. She never stuttered with other people. She considered him a giant. She never even dared to wake him.

The Birthday Gift

One day, the grandmother informed Kezia that father's birthday was next week. She suggested that she should make him a pin-cushion for a gift out of a beautiful piece of yellow silk. Laboriously, with a double cotton, the little girl stitched three sides. She now needed something to fill it with. On the bed-table she discovered a great many sheets of fine paper, gathered them up, tore them into tiny pieces and stuffed her case, then sewed up the fourth side.

Hysteria in the House

That night there was a hue and cry in the house. Father's great speech for the Port Authority had been lost. Finally mother came to Kezia and asked her if she had seen the papers. The poor child replied that she had tore them up. The father beat her with a ruler. She told him that it was for his birthday. Later that night, Kezia was so upset that she wished that there were no fathers. Kezia was more afraid of him from thereafter.

The Father Next Door

The Macdonalds lived next door. They had five children. Looking through a gap in the fence the little girl saw them playing in the evening. The father with the baby, on his shoulders, two little girls hanging on to his coat pockets ran round and round the flower-beds, shaking with laughter. Once she saw the boys turn the hose on him—and he tried to catch them laughing all the time. Kezia thought that there were different sorts of father.

Kezia' Feelings Change

The mother fell ill and the grandmother went to the hospital along with her. Kezia was afraid. She was thinking about the nightmares she used to have. The night came and with it came a nightmare. She woke up shivering only to find her father beside her bed. She told him about the nightmare. The father carried Kezia to his room. He tucked her in his bed. Kezia was at peace now. She remembered her mistake and thought that her father was too tired to be Macdonald every day. She had started loving her father.

Exercises

Thinking about the Text

I. *Given below are some emotions that Kezia felt. Match the emotions in Column A with the items in Column B.*

	A		B
1.	fear or terror	(i)	father comes into her room to give her a goodbye kiss
2.	glad sense of relief	(ii)	noise of the carriage grows fainter
3.	a 'funny' feeling, perhaps of understanding	(iii)	father comes home
		(iv)	speaking to father
		(v)	going to bed when alone at home
		(vi)	father comforts her and falls asleep
		(vii)	father stretched out on the sofa, snoring

Ans.

	A		B
		(iii)	father comes home
		(iv)	speaking to father
1.	fear or terror	(v)	going to bed when alone at home
		(vii)	father stretched out on the sofa snoring
2.	glad sense of relief	(i)	father comes into her room to give her a goodbye kiss
		(ii)	noise of the carriage grows fainter
3.	a 'funny' feeling, perhaps of understanding	(vi)	father comforts her and falls asleep

II. *Answer the following questions in one or two sentences.*

1. Why was Kezia afraid of her father?
2. Who were the people in Kezia's family?
3. What was Kezia's father's routine
   (*i*) before going to his office?
   (*ii*) after coming back from his office?
   (*iii*) on Sundays?
4. In what ways did Kezia's grandmother encourage her to get to know her father better?

Ans. 1. Kezia was afraid of her father because she always looked at him as someone who scolded her and told her to do things properly. He never played with her and looked like a giant.

2. Kezia's family consisted of her mother, father and grandmother.

3. (*i*) Kezia's father usually went into her room to give her a casual kiss.

   (*ii*) He asked in a loud voice to bring him tea, newspaper and his slippers.

   (*iii*) He slept soundly while being stretched out on the sofa, with a handkerchief covering his face.

4. On Sundays, Kezia's grandmother sent her to the drawing room to have a talk with her parents. The grandmother also encourages Kezia to make a gift for her father's birthday.

III. *Discuss these questions in class with your teacher and then write down your answers in two or three paragraphs each.*

1. Kezia's efforts to please her father resulted in displeasing him very much. How did this happen?
2. Kezia decides that there are "different kinds of fathers". What kind of father was Mr Macdonald and how was he different from Kezia's father?
3. How does Kezia begin to see her father as a human being who needs her sympathy?

Ans. 1. Once, Kezia's grandmother told her that her father's birthday was nearing. She also suggested that Kezia should make a pin-cushion as a gift for her father's birthday. Kezia started making the cushion and had stitched three sides. Now, she needed something to fill it with. She found many sheets of fine paper on the bed table. She gathered the sheets, tore them into tiny pieces and stuffed the cushion.

Unfortunately, the sheets were her father's speech for the Port Authority. Her father was so angry with her that he beat her with a ruler. Hence, Kezia's efforts to please her father resulted in displeasing him very much.

2. Kezia was upset after the beating. Once, she looked through a gap in the fence in the evening, she saw the Macdonalds playing 'tag' together. Mr Macdonald was playing with his children. This was when she decided that there were different sorts of fathers.

   Unlike Mr Macdonald, Kezia's father never played or laughed with her. She was too afraid to go near him and stammered in front of him.

3. When her grandmother and mother were in the hospital, Kezia was left alone at home with the cook, Alice. She wondered how she would spend the night. She used to have nightmares.

   She had the same nightmare that night and cried out her grandmother's name. When she woke up, she saw her father beside her bed. He picked her up and took her to his room. He tucked up close to her. He also told her to warm her feet.

   It was then that she realised some new thing about him. She realised that there was no one to look after him. She understood that he had to work every day and was too tired to be like Mr Macdonald. She felt bad that she had torn up his speech.

Thinking about Language

I. *Glad, happy, pleased, delighted, thrilled and overjoyed are synonyms (words or expressions that have the same or nearly the same meaning.) However, they express happiness in certain ways.*

1. Use an appropriate word from the synonyms given above in the following sentences. Clues are given in brackets.

   (*i*) She was __________ by the news of her brother's wedding. (very pleased)

   (*ii*) I was __________ to be invited to the party. (extremely pleased and excited about) (*iii*) She was __________ at the birth of her granddaughter. (extremely happy)

(*iv*) The coach was __________ with his performance. (satisfied about)

(*v*) She was very __________ with her results. (happy about something that has happened)

Ans. (*i*) She was thrilled by the news of her brother's wedding.

(*ii*) I was delighted to be invited to the party.

(*iii*) She was overjoyed at the birth of her granddaughter.

(*iv*) The coach was pleased with his performance.

(*v*) She was very happy with her results.

2. Study the use of the word *big* in the following sentence.
He was so *big*- his hands and his neck, especially his mouth...
Here, *big* means *large in size*.
Now, consult a dictionary and find out the meaning of *big* in the following sentences. The first one has been done for you.

(*i*) You are a big girl now. <u>*older*</u>

(*ii*) Today you are going to take the biggest decision of your career. __________

(*iii*) Their project is full of big ideas. __________

(*iv*) Cricket is a big game in our country. __________

(*v*) I am a big fan of Lata Mangeskar. __________

(*vi*) You have to cook a bit more as my friend is a big eater. __________

(*vii*) What a big heart you've got, Father dear. __________

Ans. (*i*) Older
(*ii*) Most important
(*iii*) Excellent ideas
(*iv*) Huge in popularity
(*v*) Greatest
(*vi*) Eats a lot (in quantity)
(*vii*) A good and kind heart

II. *Verbs of Reporting*

1. Underline the verbs of reporting in the following sentences.

(*i*) He says he will enjoy the ride.

(*ii*) Father mentioned that he was going on a holiday.

(*iii*) No one told us that the shop was closed.

(*iv*) He answered that the price would go up.

(*v*) I wondered why he was screaming.

(*vi*) Ben told her to wake him up.

(*vii*) Ratan apologised for coming late to the party.

Ans. (*i*) He says he will enjoy the ride.

(*ii*) Father mentioned that he was going on a holiday.

(*iii*) No one told us that the shop was closed.

(*iv*) He answered that the price would go up.

(*v*) I wondered why he was screaming.

(*vi*) Ben told her to wake him up.

(*vii*) Ratan apologised for coming late to the party.

2. Some verbs of reporting are given in the box. Choose the appropriate verbs and fill in the blanks in the following sentences.

were complaining	shouted	replied
remarked	ordered	suggested

(*i*) "I am not afraid," __________ the woman.

(*ii*) "Leave me alone," my mother __________.

(*iii*) The children __________ that the roads were crowded and noisy.

(*iv*) "Perhaps he isn't a bad sort of a chap after all," __________ the master.

(*v*) "Let's go and look at the school ground," __________ the sports teacher.

(*vi*) The traffic police __________ all the passers-by to keep off the road.

Ans. (*i*) "I am not afraid," remarked the woman.

(*ii*) "Leave me alone," my mother shouted.

(*iii*) The children were complaining that the roads were crowded and noisy.

(*iv*) "Perhaps he isn't a bad sort of a chap after all," replied the man.

(*v*) "Let's go and look at the school ground," suggested the sports teacher.

(*vi*) The traffic police ordered all the passers-by to keep off the road.

4

A Truly Beautiful Mind

Chapter Sketch

The story of Einstein tries to show him as a human being, a fairly ordinary person who had his likes and dislikes, his streaks of rebellion and his problems. It gives an insight into his personal and professional life.

Detailed Summary

Not Very Bright from Birth

Albert Einstein was born on 14 March 1879 in the German city of Ulm, without any indication that he was destined for greatness. He was considered a freak by his own mother as his head seemed too large. Einstein started talking late and when he did, he repeated everything twice. His playmates called him "Brother Boring". But he loved mechanical toys.

Not a Bad Pupil

A headmaster told his father that Einstein would never have success at anything. He learned to play the violin. He was not a bad pupil though. He scored good marks in almost every subject, but he hated the school regimentation. At the age of 15, he left school for good.

Einstein's Interests

Einstein was highly gifted in Mathematics and interested in Physics and after finishing school, he decided to study at a university in Zurich. There is fell in love with a fellow student, Mileva Maric. He found her to be a "clever creature".

Einstein Starts Working

He worked as a teaching assistant, gave private tuitions and finally secured a job in 1902 as a technical assistant. While he was supposed to be assessing other people's inventions, Einstein was actually developing his own ideas in secret. He is said to have jokingly called his desk drawer at work the "Bureau of Theoretical Physics".

One of the famous papers of 1905 was Einstein's 'Special Theory of Relativity,' according to which time and distance are not absolute. From this followed the world's most famous formula which describes the relationship between mass and energy

$$E = mc^2$$

[In this mathematical equation, E stands for energy, m for mass and c for the speed of the light in a vacuum (about 300,000 km/s)].

Troubles of Personal Life

Albert wanted to marry Mileva but his mother was against it. Finally the couple married in January 1903 and had two sons only to drift apart a few years later in 1919. Einstein married his cousin Elsa the same year.

Another Great Achievement

In 1915, he had published his 'General Theory of Relativity,' which provided a new interpretation of gravity. The newspapers proclaimed his work as "a scientific revolution." Einstein received the Nobel Prize for Physics in 1921. He was showered with honours and invitations from all over the world and lauded by the press.

A Humanitarian

After the Nazis came to power in Germany in 1933, Einstein emigrated to the United States. They discovered nuclear fission and the danger to use of an atomic bomb loomed large over the world. Einstein wrote to American President, Franklin D. Roosevelt, on 2 August 1939, in which he warned about the destruction such a bomb could cause. The Americans developed the atomic bomb in a secret project of their own and dropped it on the Japanese cities of Hiroshima and Nagasaki in August 1945.

Einstein was deeply shaken by the extent of the destruction. For years to come, he worked for peace and world brotherhood. He died in 1955 at the age of 76.

Exercises

Thinking about the Text

Q1. Here are some headings for paragraphs in the text. Write the number(s) of the paragraph(s) for each title against the heading. The first one is done for you.

(*i*) Einstein's equation
(*ii*) Einstein meets his future wife
(*iii*) The making of a violinist
(*iv*) Mileva and Einstein's mother
(*v*) A letter that launched the arms race
(*vi*) A desk drawer full of ideas
(*vii*) Marriage and divorce

Ans. (*i*) 9 (*ii*) 7
(*iii*) 3 (*iv*) 10
(*v*) 15 (*vi*) 8
(*vii*) 11

Q2. Who had these opinions about Einstein?

(i) He was boring.
(ii) He was stupid and would never succeed in life.
(iii) He was a freak.

Ans. (*i*) Einstein's playmates.
(*ii*) Einstein's headmaster.
(*iii*) Einstein's mother.

Q3. Explain what the reasons for the following are.

(*i*) Einstein leaving the school in Munich for good.

(*ii*) Einstein wanting to study in Switzerland rather than in Munich.

(*iii*) Einstein seeing in Mileva an ally.

(*iv*) What do these tell you about Einstein?

Ans. (*i*) Einstein hated the regimentation of school. As a result, he often had clashes with his teachers. At the age of 15, when he felt too stifled to continue studying, he left the school in Munich for good.

(*ii*) Switzerland was more liberal than Munich. Hence, he wanted to study in Switzerland.

(*iii*) Einstein thought that she was a very "clever creature". He was fascinated by her.

(*iv*) These incidents show that Einstein was very clear about the things which he wanted in his life. He was goal oriented. He was also an visionary who could easily interpret the things to come.

Q4. What did Einstein call his desk drawer at the patent office? Why?

Ans. Einstein called his desk drawer at the patent office the "Bureau of Theoretical Physics". He gave it this name because while he was supposed to be assessing other people's inventions, he was actually developing his own ideas in secret and his drawer was where he stored these ideas.

Q5. Why did Einstein write a letter to Franklin Roosevelt?

Ans. The Nazis had discovered the knowledge to create atomic bombs. The American physicists feared that the Nazis could now build and use an atomic bomb. When one of his colleagues urged him, Einstein wrote a letter to Franklin Roosevelt to warn him of the destruction that could be brought by such a bomb.

Q6. How did Einstein react to the bombing of Hiroshima and Nagasaki?

Ans. Einstein was deeply shaken by the extent of the destruction caused by the explosions of atomic bombs in the Japanese cities of Hiroshima and Nagasaki. He proposed the formation of a world government. After his plea went unheard, he engaged himself in politics and indulged himself to work for world peace and disarmament.

Q7. Why does the world remember Einstein as a "world citizen"?

Ans. The world remembers Einstein as a "world citizen" because he not only made many discoveries in science, which have helped the human race immensely, but also that he was deeply concerned world peace. He tried to benefit humanity in every way he could.

Q8. Here are some facts from Einstein's life. Arrange them in chronological order.

(*i*) Einstein publishes his special theory of relativity.
(*ii*) He is awarded the Nobel Prize in Physics.
(*iii*) Einstein writes a letter to US President, Franklin D Roosevelt and warns against Germany's building of an atomic bomb.
(*iv*) Einstein attends a high school in Munich.
(*v*) Einstein family moves to Milan.
(*vi*) Einstein is born in the German city of Ulm.
(*vii*) Einstein joins a university in Zurich, where he meets Mileva.
(*viii*) Einstein dies.
(*ix*) He provides a new interpretation of gravity.
(*x*) Tired of the school's regimentation, Einstein withdraws from school.
(*xi*) He works in a patent office as a technical expert.
(*xii*) When Hitler comes to power, Einstein leaves Germany for the United States.

Ans. (*i*) Einstein is born in the German city of Ulm.
(*ii*) Einstein attends a high school in Munich.
(*iii*) Einstein's family moves to Milan.
(*iv*) Tired of the school's regimentation, Einstein withdraws from school.
(*v*) Einstein joins a university in Zurich, where he meets Mileva.
(*vi*) He works in a patent office as a technical expert.
(*vii*) Einstein publishes his special theory of relativity.
(*viii*) He provides a new interpretation of gravity.
(*ix*) He is awarded the Nobel Prize in Physics.

(*x*) When Hitler comes to power, Einstein leaves Germany for the United States.

(*xi*) Einstein writes a letter to US President, Franklin D Roosevelt, and warns against Germany's building of an atomic bomb.

(*xii*) Einstein dies.

Thinking about Language

I. *Here are some sentences from the story. Choose the word from the brackets which can be substituted for the italicised words in the sentences.*

(*i*) A few years later, the marriage *faltered*. (failed, broke, became weak)

(*ii*) Einstein was constantly *at odds* with people at the university. (on bad terms, in disagreement, unhappy)

(*iii*) The newspapers *proclaimed* his work as "a scientific revolution." (declared, praised, showed)

(*iv*) Einstein got ever more involved in politics, *agitating* for an end to the arms build-up. (campaigning, fighting, supporting)

(*v*) At the age of 15, Einstein felt so stifled that he left the school *for good*, (permanently, for his benefit, for a short time)

(*vi*) Five years later, the discovery of nuclear fission in Berlin had American physicists *in an uproar*. (in a state of commotion, full of criticism, in a desperate state)

(*vii*) Science wasn't the only thing that *appealed to* the dashing young man with the walrus moustache. (interested, challenged, worried)

Ans. (*i*) Failed

(*ii*) In disagreement

(*iii*) Declared

(*iv*) Campaigning

(*v*) Permanently

(*vi*) In a state of commotion

(*vii*) Interested

II. *Complete the sentences below by filling in the blanks with suitable participal clauses. The information that has to be used in the phrases is provided as a sentence in brackets.*

1. ...., the firefighters finally put out the fire. (They worked round the clock.)
2. She watched the sunset above the mountain, ... (She noticed the colours blending softly into one another.)
3. The excited horse pawed the ground rapidly, ... (While it neighed continually.)
4. ...., I found myself in Bengaluru, instead of Benaras. (I had taken the wrong train.)
5. ...., I was desperate to get to the bathroom. (I had not bathed for two days.)
6. The stone steps, ... needed to be replaced.(They were worn down.)
7. The actor received hundreds of letters from his fans, __________ (They asked him to send them his photograph.)

Ans.
1. Working round the clock, the firefighters finally put out the fire.
2. Noticing the colours blending softly into one another, she watched the sunset above the mountain.
3. The excited horse pawed the ground rapidly, neighing continually.
4. Having taken the wrong train, I found myself in Bengaluru, instead of Benaras.
5. Having not bathed for two days, I was desperate to get to the bathroom.
6. The stone steps, being worn down, needed to be replaced.
7. The actor received hundreds of letters from his fans, asking him to send them his photograph.

5

The Snake and the Mirror

Vaikom Muhammad Basheer

Chapter Sketch

The story revolves around a young doctor. He was alone at home when he had the worst experience of his life. A cobra fell on him. The horror froze him. But the snake didn't bite him. It went to look at itself in the mirror.

Detailed Summary

The Poor Doctor

It was a hot summer night. The doctor returned home after having a meal at a restaurant. As he entered the house, he heard a sound. It was due to the snakes probably. He lighted the kerosene lamp as the rented room was not electrified. His earnings were meager.

The Doctor's Musings

The doctor could not sleep and hence started reading a book. He was tempted to look into the mirror. In those days he was a great admirer of beauty and believed in making himself look handsome. He made an important decision- shave daily and grow a thin moustache to look more handsome. Then he again made a decision- to always keep that attractive smile on his face ... to look more handsome.

Finally he decided that he would marry a fat girl- who would be a rich doctor- so that she could not catch him after he makes a silly mistake and runs away.

The Horrific Encounter

With such thoughts, he again sat down. Suddenly, the cobra fell on him. He didn't move or make a noise. He was stoned by the horror. The snake slithered along his shoulder and coiled around his left arm above the elbow. The hood was spread out and its head was hardly three or four inches from his face! The doctor started praying to God. But he dare not move.

The Snake didn't Bite Him

The snake turned its head. It looked into the mirror and saw its reflection. The snake unwound itself from his arm and slowly slithered into his lap. From there it crept onto the table and moved towards the mirror. Perhaps it wanted to enjoy its reflection at closer quarters. The doctor ran straight out to his friend's home where he bathed.

The Doctor got Robbed

The next day he returned with some of his friends only to find that he had been robbed. Some thief had taken all his belongings, but left his dirty vest. The doctor was quite offended at this. He never saw the snake again. Nor he married a fat girl. He actually married a sprinter.

Exercises

Thinking about the Text

I. *Discuss in pairs and answer each question below in a short paragraph (30-40 words).*

1. "The sound was familiar one." What sound did the doctor hear? What did he think it was? How many times did he hear it? (Find the places in the text.) When and why did the sounds stop?

2. What two "important" and "earth-shaking" decisions did the doctor take while he was looking into the mirror?

3. "I looked into the mirror and smiled," says the doctor. A little later he says, "I forgot my danger and smiled feebly at myself." What is the doctor's opinion about himself when
   (*i*) he first smiles and
   (*ii*) he smiles again? In what way do his thoughts change in between and why?

Ans. 1. The doctor heard a familiar rustling sound caused by the movement of rats. He heard the sound three times and then it stopped. The next sound that he heard was a dull thud as if a rubber tube had fallen to the ground. It was a snake. The rats had stopped moving because they were afraid.

2. The first "important" decision that he took was that he would shave daily and grow a thin moustache to look more handsome. The second "earth-shaking" decision he took was that he would always keep his attractive smile on his face to look more handsome.

3. The doctor was appreciating his attractive smile when he was smiling first. His opinion about himself was that he was handsome and an eligible bachelor. Later, when he smiled feebly at himself, he had forgotten his danger. At that moment, his opinion about himself was that he was a poor, foolish and stupid doctor.

   His thoughts had changed because of the critical danger he was in.

II. *This story about a frightening incident is narrated in a humorous way. What makes it humorous? (Think of the contrasts it presents between dreams and reality. Some of them are listed below.)*

1. (*i*) The kind of person the doctor is (money, possessions)
   (*ii*) The kind of person he wants to be (appearance, ambition)

2. (*i*) The person he wants to marry
   (*ii*) The person he actually marries

3. (*i*) His thoughts when he looks into the mirror

(*ii*) His thoughts when the snake is coiled around his arm

Write short paragraphs on each of these to get your answer.

Ans. 1. (*i*) The doctor had just started his practice. His earnings were low which is evident from the fact that the small rented room in which he lived was not even electrified. Moreover, it was infested with rats. He had only sixty rupees in his suitcase. He had one solitary black coat. So, he is not a man of possessions or money.

(*ii*) The doctor wants to be rich. He also would like to have a good appearance. The life which he wants to live is in complete contrast to this. He thought he was handsome and a doctor which made him an eligible bachelor. The manner in which he describes his "earth-shaking" decisions to look handsome is indeed humorous.

2. (*i*) The doctor wants to marry a woman doctor who was rich and had a good medical practice. He wanted a fat wife so that whenever he would make a mistake his wife would not be able to catch him.

(*ii*) The woman he marries was a thin reddy woman and ran like a sprinter. He find his smile attractive. This is another humorous contrast.

3. (*i*) He admired his smile and beauty when he looked into the mirror easily. He decided that the smile added to his good looks and thus he should always wear it. These decision, he describes, are "important" and "earth-shaking".

(*ii*) When the snake was coiled around his arm, he turned into a stone. He realised that if the snake bit him, then he did not even have any anti-venom medicines in his room. That was when he thought that he was a poor, foolish and stupid doctor. From an eligible bachelor to a foolish stupid guy, the way he explains this and emphasis his "earth-shaking" decisions make it humorous.

Thinking about Language

I. *Here are some sentences from the text. Say which of them tell you, that the author (a) was afraid of the snake, (b) was proud of his appearance, (c) had a sense of humour, (d) was no longer afraid of the snake.*

1. I was turned to stone.
2. I was no mere image cut in granite.
3. The arm was beginning to be drained of strength.
4. I tried in my imagination to write in bright letters outside my little heart the words, 'O God'.
5. I didn't tremble. I didn't cry out.
6. I looked into the mirror and smiled. It was an attractive smile.
7. I was suddenly a man of flesh and blood.
8. I was after all a bachelor and a doctor too on top of it!
9. The fellow had such a sense of cleanliness...! The rascal could have taken it and used it after washing it with soap and water.
10. Was it trying to make an important decision about growing a moustache or using eye shadow and mascara or wearing a vermilion spot on its forehead.

Ans. The following sentences tell that the author

(a) was afraid of the snake (1), (3), (4), (5)

(b) was proud of his appearance (6), (8)

(c) had a sense of humour (9), (10)

(d) was no longer afraid of the snake: (2), (7)

II. *Expressions used to show fear*

Can you find the expressions in the story that tell you that the author was frightened? Read the story and complete the following sentences.

1. I was turned ________________________________.
2. I sat there holding ____________________________.
3. In the light of the lamp I sat there like ______________.

Ans. 1. I was turned to stone.
2. I sat there holding my breath.
3. In the light of the lamp I sat there like a stone image in the flesh.

III. *In the sentences given below some words and expressions are italicised. They variously mean that one*

- is very frightened.
- is too scared to move.
- is frightened by something that happens suddenly.
- makes another feel frightened.

Match the meanings with the words/expressions in italics and write the appropriate meaning next to the sentence. The first one has been done for you.

1. I knew a man was following me, I was *scared out of my wits*. (very frightened)
2. I *got a fright* when I realised how close I was to the cliff edge.
3. He *nearly jumped out of his skin* when he saw the bull coming towards him.
4. You really *gave me a fright* when you crept up behind me like that.
5. Wait until I tell his story - it will *make your hair stand on* end.
6. *Paralysed with fear*, the boy faced his abductors.
7. The boy hid behind the door, *not moving a muscle*.

Ans. 1. Very frightened
2. Frightened by something that happens suddenly
3. Frightened by something that happens suddenly
4. Frightened by something that happens suddenly
5. Makes another feel frightened
6. Too scared to move
7. Too scared to move

IV. *Reported Questions*

Report these questions using if/whether or why/ when/ where/ how/which/what. Remember the italicised verbs change into the past tense.

1. Meena asked her friend, "*Do* you *think* your teacher will come today?"
2. David asked his colleague, "Where *will* you go this summer?"
3. He asked the little boy, "Why *are* you studying English?"
4. She asked me, "When *are* we going to leave?"
5. Pran asked me, "*Have* you finished reading the newspaper?"
6. Seema asked her, "How long *have* you lived here?"
7. Sheila asked the children "*Are* you ready to do the work?"

Ans.

1. Meena asked her friend if she thought her teacher would come that day.
2. David asked his colleague where he would go that summer.
3. He asked the little boy why he was studying English.
4. She asked me when we were going to leave.
5. Pran asked me if I had finished reading the newspaper.
6. Seema asked her how long she had lived there.
7. Sheila asked the children if they were ready to do the work.

6

My Childhood

APJ Abdul Kalam

Chapter Sketch

"My Childhood" is an extract taken from "Wings of Fire". The chapter is a journey of young Abdul Kalam. Kalam speaks about his childhood, the stigma of cast and the barriers he overcame on the way to become the thirteenth President of India. He also talks about friends and teachers who supported him on his journey.

Detailed Summary

Early Childhood of Kalam

Kalam was born into a middle-class Tamil family in the island town of Rameswaram in the erstwhile Madras State to a generous father, Jainulabdeen and a loving mother, Ashiamma. They lived in a fairly large ancestral house and Kalam feels that they provided for more mouths than in their family. Kalam also says that his was a very secure childhood, both materially and emotionally.

Kalam did Small Chores to Earn Money

After the Second World War broke out in 1939, a sudden demand for tamarind seeds erupted in the market. Kalam used to sell these seeds and earn one anna. Their area was a bit isolated and hence was not affected by the war. But when India was forced to join the war, the first thing that happened was the suspension of the train halt at Rameswaram station. The newspapers now had to be bundled and thrown out from the moving train on the Rameswaram Road between Rameswaram and Dhanuskodi. That forced his cousin Samsuddin, who distributed newspapers in Rameswaram, to look for a helping hand to catch the bundles and Kalam filled the slot. In this way, Samsuddin helped Kalam earn his first wages.

Kalam's Friends

He inherited honesty and self discipline from his father; from his mother, he inherited faith in goodness and deep kindness. He had three close friends in his childhood - Ramanadha Sastry, Aravindan and Sivaprakasan. All these boys were from orthodox Hindu Brahmin families. Ramanadha Sastry was the son of Pakshi Lakshmana Sastry, the high priest of the Rameswaram temple.

Kalam First Brush with Casteism

One day, in fifth standard, a new teacher came to their class. Kalam was wearing a cap and was sitting with Ramanadha Sastry. The new teacher could not stomach a Hindu priest's son sitting with a Muslim boy. He asked Kalam to go and sit on the back bench. They narrated the incident to their parents. Lakshmana Sastry summoned the teacher and told the teacher that he should not spread the poison of social inequality and communal intolerance in the minds of innocent children. He bluntly asked the teacher to either apologise or quit the school and the island. Not only did the teacher regret his behaviour, but the strong sense of conviction Lakshmana Sastry conveyed ultimately reformed this young teacher.

Another Incident of Social Inequality

His science teacher Sivasubramania Iyer, though an orthodox Brahmin with a very conservative wife, was something of a rebel. He used to spend hours with Kalam and wanted him to develop to be at par with the people of cities. One day, he invited him to his home for a meal. His wife was horrified at the idea of a Muslim boy being invited to dine in her ritually pure kitchen. She refused to serve me in her kitchen. His teacher served him. His teacher again invited him to dinner. He wanted him to change the system and fight such things. On dinner, his teacher's wife herself served him.

Abdul Wanted to Pursue Higher Studies

Abdul asked his father's permission to go out of the village and pursue higher studies. His mother was emotional but his father knew that he had to leave. He quoted Kahil Gibran and tried to console his mother. He told her that the children had the right to follow their dreams.

Thinking about the Text

I. *Answer these questions in one or two sentences each.*

Q 1. Where was Abdul Kalam's house?

Ans. Abdul Kalam's house was situated in Rameswaram in the erstwhile Madras state.

Q 2. What do you think *Dinamani* is the name of? Give a reason for your answer.

Ans. *Dinamani* was most probably the name of a newspaper. Abdul Kalam tried to trace the stories of the Second World War in the headlines in Dinamani.

Q 3. Who were Abdul Kalam's school friends? What did they later become?

Ans. Abdul Kalam had three close friends in school Ramanadha Sastry, Aravindan and Sivaprakasan. Ramanadha Sastry became the priest of the Rameswaram temple. Aravindan started a business of arranging transport for visiting pilgrims. Sivaprakasan became a catering contractor for the Southern Railways.

Q 4. How did Abdul Kalam earn his first wages?

Ans. He earned his first wages by providing a helping hand to his cousin, Samsuddin. He used to catch the newspaper bundles for him from the moving train.

Q 5. Had he earned any money before that? In what way?

Ans. Yes, he did it by selling the tamarind seeds in the market. He earned an anna daily.

II. *Answer each of these questions in a short paragraph (about 30 words).*

Q 1. How does the author describe (i) his father, (ii) his mother, (iii) himself?

Ans. (*i*) Kalam describes his father, Jainulabdeen, as a simple man. He neither had much formal education nor much wealth. But he possessed great innate wisdom and a true generosity of spirit. He also avoided all inessential comforts and luxuries.

(*ii*) Kalam's mother, Ashiamma was an ideal helpmate to her husband. She used to feed many people everyday. She is also emotional which is clear from her sadness when Kalam decides to leave his home for further studies.

(*iii*) The author describes himself as one of many children. Though his parents were tall and handsome, he was a short boy with rather undistinguished looks. He had a very secure childhood, both materially and emotionally.

***Q* 2.** What characteristics does he say he inherited from his parents?

Ans. The author inherited honesty and self-discipline from his father and faith in goodness and deep kindness from his mother.

III. ***Discuss these questions in class with your teacher and then write down your answers in two or three paragraphs each.***

***Q* 1.** "On the whole, the small society of Rameswaram was very rigid in terms of the segregation of different social groups," says the author.

(*i*) Which social groups does he mention? Were these groups easily identifiable (for example, by the way they dressed)?

(*ii*) Were they aware only of their differences or did they also naturally share friendships and experiences? (Think of the bedtime stories in Kalam's house; of who his friends were; and of what used to take place in the pond near his house.)

(*iii*) The author speaks both of people who were very aware of the differences among them and those who tried to bridge these differences. Can you identify such people in the text?

(*iv*) Narrate two incidents that show how differences can be created, and also how they can be resolved. How can people change their attitudes?

Ans. (*i*) Kalam mentions two social groups—the Hindus and the Muslims. Yes, these groups were easily identifiable. The Hindus wore a sacred thread and the Muslims wore a cap.

(*ii*) Abdul Kalam was Muslim and his friends were from orthodox Hindu Brahmin families. But they were very close friends. It means that though they were aware of their cultural differences, they naturally shared friendships and experiences. During the annual Shri Sita Rama Kalyanam ceremony, Kalam's family arranged boats with a special platform for carrying idols of the Lord from the temple to the marriage site. His grandmother narrated events from the Ramayana and from the life of the Prophet as bedtime stories. All these incidents show that different social groups naturally co-inhabited Rameswaram.

(*iii*) Kalam describes two people who were very critical of the differences among them. One was the new teacher who came to the class when Kalam was in the fifth standard and did not let him sit with Ramanadha Sastry who was a Brahmin. The other was the wife of his science teacher, Sivasubramania Iyer.

She did not allow Kalam to eat in her pure Hindu kitchen. The people who tried to bridge these differences were Lakshmana Sastry, a priest and the father of Kalam's friend Ramanadha and Sivasubramania Iyer.

(*iv*) When Kalam was in the fifth standard, a new teacher came to their class. The teacher could not digest the fact that a Hindu priest's son, Ramanadha was sitting with a Muslim boy. Abdul Kalam. The teacher immediately sent Kalam to sit on the back bench.

Both the boys narrated this story to their respective parents. Lakshmana Sastry summoned the teacher and told him that he should not spread the venom of social inequality and communal intolerance in the minds of innocent children. He asked the teacher to apologise of to leave the place that instant.

Once, Kalam's science teacher, Sivasubramania Iyer, invited him for a meal to his house. His wife was horrified at the idea of a Muslim boy eating in her pure Hindu kitchen. She refused to serve him. But Iyer served Kalam with his own hands and sat down beside him to eat his meal.

Sivasubramania Iyer again invited him for dinner the next weekend. Obviously Kalam was apprehensive. Iyer told him that if one has decided to change the system, such problems have to be confronted with. When Kalam visited the house next week, Sivasubramania Iyer's wife took him inside her kitchen and served him food with her own hands.

Differences can be resolved and people's attitudes can be changed if we don't pollute our minds with communal intolerance and think rationally.

Q 2. (*i*) Why did Abdul Kalam want to leave Rameswaram?
(*ii*) What did his father say to this?
(*iii*) What do you think his words mean? Why do you think he spoke those words?

Ans. (*i*) Kalam wanted to leave Rameswaram for further studies. He wanted to study at the district headquarters in Ramanathapuram.

(*ii*) His father said that he knew that one day Kalam had to go away to grow. He talked about the seagull that flies across the sun alone and without a nest. He then quoted Khalil Gibran to Kalam's mother saying that nobody's children were their own children. They were the sons and daughters of Life's longing for itself. They come through their parents, but not from them. They may give them their love, but not their thoughts. For they have their own thoughts.

(*iii*) His words mean that there comes a point on our lives when we have to leave behind our loved ones in order to grow and give direction to our lives. Parents have the duty to nurture their child but they cannot force their thoughts on them. Children have their own thoughts and lives. Kalam's father spoke these words because Kalam's mother was hesitant about Kalam's decision to leave his house for further studies.

Thinking about Language

I. *Find the sentences in the text where these words occur*

erupt	surge	trace	undistinguished	casualty

Look these words up in a dictionary which gives examples of how they are used. Now answer the following questions.

Q 1. What are the things that can *erupt*? Use examples to explain the various meanings of *erupt*. Now do the same for the word *surge*. What things can *surge*?

Ans. *Things that can erupt are* Volcanoes, anger, emotions etc.

For example, His anger erupted when he saw that his stuff was misplaced.

Things that can surge are Waves, floods, demands, popularity etc.

For example, The flood came in darkness, with a sudden surge of water.

Q 2. What are the meanings of the word *trace* and which of the meanings is closest to the word in the text?

Ans. *The following are the meanings of the word trace*

(*i*) Follow, discover or ascertain the course of development of something.

(*ii*) Make a mark or lines on a surface.

(*iii*) To go back over again.

(*iv*) Pursue or chase relentlessly.

(*v*) Find or discover through investigation.

(*vi*) Make one's course or travel along a path; travel or pass over, around or along.

(*vii*) Read with difficulty.

The closest meaning of the word 'trace' in the text is 'to find or discover through investigation'.

Q 3. Can you find the word *undistinguished* in your dictionary? (If not, look up the word *distinguished* and say what *undistinguished* must mean.)

Ans. Yes, the word undistinguished exists in the dictionary.

The following are different meanings along with usage

(*i*) (*a*) Marked by no peculiar quality; not distinguished; ordinary an *undistinguished appearance.*

(*b*) Lacking particularly good qualities; mediocre *an undistinguished performance.*

(*ii*) Not separated from others into categories.

(*iii*) Unnoticed; unperceived *an undistinguished face in the crowd.*

II. **1. Match the phrases in Column A with their meanings in Column B.**

A	B
(i) broke out	(a) an attitude of kindness, a readiness to give freely
(ii) in accordance with	(b) was not able to tolerate
(iii) a helping hand	(c) began suddenly in a violent way
(iv) could not stomach	(d) assistance
(v) generosity of spirit	(e) persons with power to make decisions
(vi) figures of authority	(f) according to a particular rule, principle or system

Ans.

A	B
(i) broke out	(c) began suddenly in a violent way
(ii) in accordance with	(f) according to a particular rule, principle or system
(iii) a helping hand	(d) assistance
(iv) could not stomach	(b) was not able to tolerate
(v) generosity of spirit	(a) an attitude of kindness, a readiness to give freely
(vi) figures of authority	(e) persons with power to make decisions

2. *Form the opposites of the words below by prefixing un- or in-. The prefix in- can also have the forms il-, ir-, or im- (for example illiterate –il + literate, impractical –im + practical, irrational ir + rational). You may consult a dictionary if you wish.*

___ adequate	___ acceptable	___ regular	___ tolerant
___ demanding	___ active	___ true	___ permanent
___ patriotic	___ disputed	___ accessible	___ coherent
___ logical	___ legal	___ responsible	___ possible

Ans.

*In*adequate	*Un*acceptable	*Ir*regular	*In*tolerant
*Un*demanding	*In*active	*Un*true	*Im*permanent
*Un*patriotic	*Un*disputed	*In*accessible	*In*coherent
*Il*logical	*Il*legal	*Ir*responsible	*Im*possible

III. *Rewrite the sentences below, changing the verbs in brackets into the passive form.*

***Q* 1.** In yesterday's competition the prizes (give away) by the Principal.

Ans. In yesterday's competition the prizes were given away by the Principal.

***Q* 2.** In spite of financial difficulties, the labourers (pay) on time.

Ans. In spite of financial difficulties, the labourers were paid on time.

***Q* 3.** On Republic Day, vehicles (not allow) beyond this point.

Ans. On Republic Day, vehicles will not be allowed beyond this point.

***Q* 4.** Second-hand books (buy and sell) on the pavement every Saturday.

Ans. Second-hand books are bought and sold on the pavement every Saturday.

***Q* 5.** Elections to the Lok Sabha (hold) every five years.

Ans. Elections to the Lok Sabha are held every five years.

***Q* 6.** Our National Anthem (compose) Rabindranath Tagore.

Ans. Our National Anthem was composed by Rabindranath Tagore.

IV. *Rewrite the paragraphs below, using the correct form of the verb given in brackets.*

***Q* 1.** **How Helmets Came To Be Used in Cricket**

Nari Contractor was the Captain and an opening batsman for India in the 1960s. The Indian cricket team went on a tour to the West Indies in 1962. In a match against Barbados in Bridgetown, Nari Contractor (seriously injure and collapse). In those days helmets (not wear). Contractor (hit) on the head by a bouncer from Charlie Griffith. Contractor's skull (fracture). The entire team (deeply concern). The West Indies players (worry). Contractor (rush) to hospital. He (accompany) by Frank Worrell, the Captain of the West Indies Team. Blood (donate) by the West Indies players. Thanks to the timely help, Contractor (save). Nowadays helmets (routinely use) against bowlers.

Ans. **How Helmets Came To Be Used in Cricket**

Nari Contractor was the Captain and an opening batsman for India in the 1960s. The Indian cricket team went on a tour to the West Indies in 1962. In a match against Barbados in Bridgetown, Nari Contractor got seriously injured and collapsed. In those days helmets were not worn. Contractor was hit on the head by a bouncer from Charlie Griffith. Contractor's skull had been fractured. The entire team was deeply concerned. The West Indies players were worried. Contractor was rushed to hospital. He was accompanied by Frank Worrell, the Captain of the West Indies Team. Blood was donated by the West Indies players. Thanks to the timely help, Contractor was saved. Nowadays helmets are routinely usedagainst bowlers.

***Q*2. Oil From Seeds**

Vegetable oils (make) from seeds and fruits of many plants growing all over the world, from tiny sesame seeds to big, juicy coconuts. Oil (produce) from cotton seeds, groundnuts, soya beans and sunflower seeds. Olive oil (use) for cooking, salad dressing etc. Olives (shake) from the trees and (gather) up, usually by hand. The olives (ground) to a thick paste which is spread onto special mats. Then the mats (layer) up on the pressing machine which will gently squeeze them to produce olive oil.

Ans. **Oil From Seeds**

Vegetable oils are made from seeds and fruits of many plants growing all over the world, from tiny sesame seeds to big, juicy coconuts. Oil is produced from cotton seeds, groundnuts, soya beans and sunflower seeds. Olive oil is used for cooking, salad dressing etc. Olives are shaken from the trees and gathered up, usually by hand. The olives are grounded to a thick paste which is spread onto special mats. Then the mats are layered up on the pressing machine which will gently squeeze them to produce olive oil.

1

The Road Not Taken

Robert Frost

Chapter Sketch

The road in the poem is the metaphor for life. The poem suggests that we all have to take decisions in our life. Our decisions depend on our character, our thinking and our decision-making ability. Once, we have taken a decision, there is no return.

The decision shapes our future. We can never go back and change it. If the decision was taken in a haste, we can only lament what follows.

Detailed Summary

The Poet at a Fork

Once a poet was standing in a forest at the time of autumn. The point where the poet was standing had two roads diverging into the different directions. The poet tried to analyse the better path by looking as far as he could. He could see upto a point where it turned to the undergrowth.

The Poet's Decision

One of the roads looked easier to travel as many people had travelled through it. Whereas another road was too grassy and looked as if less number of travellers had passed through it. The poet decided to adopt the second road.

However, at first the poet was not sure about his decision. He said that morning falls on both the roads equally, but still nobody stepped on this roads. He was the first one for the day to move on that road. Therefore, he doubted whether he should continue or not.

The Road Not Taken

In the last stanza, the poet decided to move forward. He thought that after ages he would tell one fact of life with a sigh. It was that between two roads, he selected one road, which was less travelled by others. And this particular decision in life made all the difference in his life. It is an eternal truth and can be applicable to all human beings.

Exercises

Thinking about the Poem

Q1. Where does the traveller find himself? What problem does he face?

Ans. The traveller finds himself at an intersection of two roads in a forest. His problem is that both the roads seemed inviting him, but he couldn't decide which one to travel on to.

Q2. Discuss what these phrases mean to you.

(*i*) A yellow wood
(*ii*) It was grassy and wanted wear
(*iii*) The passing there
(*iv*) Leaves no step had trodden black
(*v*) How way leads on to way

Ans. (*i*) A forest at the time of autumn.
(*ii*) The grass had grown on the road and it seemed as if inviting people to walk on it.
(*iii*) It means walking on the road.
(*iv*) The leaves which had not been walked over.
(*v*) How one road leads to another?

Q3. Is there any difference between the two roads as the poet describes them

(i) in stanzas two and three?

(ii) in the last two lines of the poem?

Ans. (i) Yes, there is difference between the two roads as shown in the stanzas two and three. As the poet says that one was grassy and wanted wear. In the third stanzas, he says that the leaves had not been walked over.

(ii) In the last two lines the poet clearly mentions that he took the one 'less travelled by'.

Q4. What do you think the last two lines of the poem mean? (Looking back, does the poet regret his choice or accept it?)

Ans. The last two lines are the poet's contemplation. He surely regrets his decision. The poet chose the one which was the less travelled one. He thinks his decision has made all the difference and life would have been different.

Q5. (i) Have you ever had to make a difficult choice (or do you think you will have difficult choices to make)? How will you make the choice (for what reasons)?

(ii) After you have made a choice do you always think about what might have been or do you accept the reality?

Ans. The answer to the above questions depend upon the student's thinking.

However, one may form the answer as follows

(i) Yes, I had to make a difficult choice once. I was sick and had an exam the next day. I had prepared well in advance for the exam. But alas! I decided not to appear for it.

I made my choice thinking about my health. Generally, the factors that influence my choice are risk, contentment, success, etc.

(ii) Its human nature to analyse things. I always think about my decisions. They are like my guiding light. If one past choice has done me no good, I try not to follow it in the future.

2

Wind

Subramania Bharati

Chapter Sketch

In the poem 'Wind', the poet, Subramania Bharati has personified the wind. According to him, the wind has a menacing nature. When it blows strongly, it causes a lot of destruction. But he also tells us the way of making friends with it.

Detailed Summary

The Poet's Appeal

The poet appeals to the wind to come softly. He asks the wind not to break the shutter of the windows or scatter the papers. He tells the wind not to throw down the books on the shelf, but finds that the wind had already done so. The wind tore the pages of the books and it also brought rain again.

The Menacing Nature of the Wind

The poet says that the wind makes fun of the weak. Fragile crumbling houses, decaying doors, rafters, wood, bodies, lives or hearts. The wind God blows away and crushes them all. He doesn't listen to the pleas. So, the poet wages us to joint the doors firmly and to practice to firm the body. He wants us to make our hearts strong.

The Hidden Purpose

If we do all the above things, then we can be friends with the wind. The wind blows out weak fires. He makes strong fires roar and flourish. There is a hidden message in these lines. The poet wants to say that the people weak at heart are blown out by the problems of this world whereas who are strong are instead inspired by difficulties. Hence, making friends with the wind is a good thing. We praise it.

Exercises

Thinking about the Poem

Q1. What are the things the wind does in the first stanza?

Ans. In the first stanza, the wind breaks the shutters of the windows. It scatters the papers. It throws down the books down the shelf. It also tore the pages of the book.

Q2. Have you seen anybody winnow grain at home or in a paddy field? What is the word in your language for winnowing? What do people use for winnowing? (Give the words in your language, if you know them).

Ans. The answer may differ from student to student.

The students can write their answer as follows

Yes, I have seen people winnow grain. I saw it when I went to my native place last year. In our language, it is 'फटकाना'. People use blow fans.

Q3. What does the poet say the wind God winnows?

Ans. The word 'winnow' has been used very poetically here. It means that the wind God takes away or 'winnows' the weak and frail houses, doors, rafters, wood, bodies, lives and hearts.

Q4. **What should we do to make friends with the wind?**

Ans. The wind favours the strong hence we should build strong homes, joint the doors firmly, firm the body and make our hearts strong. The poet wants to say that only the strong are spared by problems.

Q5. **What do the last four lines of the poem mean to you?**

Ans. The last four lines contain a hidden message. The lines are used to say that only the strong people are able to stand the troubles that come their way. While the weak are swept away by them, the same trouble makes the strong even stronger.

Q6. **How does the poet speak to the wind—in anger or with humour? You must also have seen or heard to the wind "crumbling lives". What is your response to this? Is it like the poet's?**

Ans. The poet appears to be angry with the wind as the wind throws down his stuff. He wants the wind to come softly. Yes, I have heard of the wind "crumbling lives". My response is like that of the poet. The poet says that the wind favours the strong. If we are weak then we will always be troubled. We need to be strong.

3

Rain on the Roof

Coates Kinney

Chapter Sketch

In the poem 'Rain on the Roof', the poet describes his feelings when he hears the rain patter on the roof of his cottage. The rain is a melody of nature. It beautifies the things around us. Hearing the rain drop, the poet gets nostalgic. Several memories of childhood run through his mind.

Detailed Summary

The Poet is Lying on His Bed

The sky is covered with dark clouds which has made the atmosphere a bit humid. After which it begins to rain. The falling rain breaks the sadness and the poet feels so cosy lying in his bed. He is filled with joy. He is enjoying the sound of patter on the cottage rooftop.

The Rain Brings Back Several Memories

Every tinkle of raindrops that fall on wooden tiles over the roof of the cottage produces an echo in the poet's heart and starts a thousand fancies in his thoughts. They appear to spin the yarns of bright fanciful colours into his mind and he listens to the patter of the rain on the roof.

The Poet Remembers His Mother

The drizzle brings back the memory of the poet's mother. He gets nostalgic. He remembers how it used to be, the face of his mother when she tucked him in his bed. It appears that the poet's mother is long gone. He continues to think about her as he listens to this refraining melody which is played by the patter of rain upon the shingles of the roof.

Exercises

Thinking about the Poem

I. ***Q*1.** What do the following phrases mean to you? Discuss in class.

(*i*) Humid shadows
(*ii*) Starry spheres
(*iii*) What a bliss
(*iv*) A thousand dreamy fancies into busy being start
(*v*) A thousand recollections weave their air-threads into woof

Ans. (*i*) Dark clouds laden with water droplets.
(*ii*) The star filled clear sky at night.
(*iii*) Utmost joy or happiness experienced by the poet.
(*iv*) The poet is lost in fantasy.
(*v*) The poet is lost in his childhood memories. He is having 'a walk down the memory lane'.

***Q*2.** What does the poet like to do when it rains?

Ans. Whon it rainc, tho poot likoc to lio down in hic bod and licton to tho patter of the soft falling shower on his cottage roof. He gets lost in fantasies and memories of his past.

***Q*3.** What is the single major memory that comes to the poet? Who are the "darling dreamers" he refers to?

Ans. The single major memory that comes to the poet is the face of his mother when she used to tuck him in his bed. "Darling dreamers" are those 'children' who dreams of their mothers like the poet.

Q4. **Is the poet now a child? Is his mother still alive?**

Ans. No, the poet appears to be a grown up adult. The poet's mother is long gone. It becomes clear when he says, "As she used in years agone,".

II. **Q1.** **When you were a young child, did your mother tuck you in, as the poet's did?**

Ans. Yes, I remember my mother used to tuck me in when I was a child. She still does it sometimes when I get sick or to just make me sleep when I keep awake till late in the night.

Q2. **Do you like rain? What do you do when it rains steadily or heavily as described in the poem?**

Ans. Yes I greatly like the rain. Whether it rains steadily or heavily, I like to get soaked up in it. It just lifts my spirits when I get drenched in it.

Q3. **Does everybody have a cosy bed to lie in when it rains? Look around you and describe how different kinds of people or animals spend time, seek shelter, etc during rain.**

Ans. I don't think everybody has a cosy bed to lie in when it rains. A poor beggar lives near the main road leading to our colony. He stays in a makeshift shelter. I have seen him get wet when it rains heavily.

When animals get caught up in rain they seek shelter under trees. People, on the other hand, either run towards a shelter or enjoy getting wet in the rain. A hot tea during rain is loved by all. Some animals like the peacock also love the rain.

4

The Lake Isle of Innisfree

William Butler Yeats

Chapter Sketch

This well-known poem explores the poet's longing for the peace and tranquility of Innisfree, a place where he spent a lot of time as a boy. This poem is a lyric.

Detailed Summary

The Poet Wants to go to Innisfree

The poet says that he will get up and go to Innisfree. He would build a small cabin of clay and fence there. He will grow nine rows of beans. He would also breed honeybees and live alone in the forests.

A Beautiful Place

The poet would be at peace there. Peace in Innisfree is omnipresent. It comes with the morning. It sings with the insects. As the day passes, the purple glow of the noon sky is very beautiful to watch. The midnight is full of glittering stars. Linnets fly in the evenings.

The Poet Longs for Innisfree

The poet's heart aches to go to a peaceful place that is Innisfree. He can hear the water of the lake touch the shore even when he is in a concrete jungle. His heart longs for Innisfree from its core.

Exercises

Thinking about the Poem

I. ***Q* 1.** What kind of place is Innisfree? Think about

(*i*) the three things the poet wants to do when he goes back there (stanza 1);

(*ii*) what he hears and sees there and its effect on him (stanza 2);

(*iii*) what he hears in his "heart's core" even when he is far away from Innisfree (stanza 3);

Ans. Innisfree is a peaceful and calm place where nature is beautiful, alive and full of life.

(*i*) *The three things that the poet would do in Innisfree are*

(a) He will build a small cabin there.

(b) He would plant nine rows of beans.

(c) He would also breed bees.

(*ii*) He hears the insects singing and the purple glow of the sky. The midnight sky is filled with glittering stars and the linnet's fly in the evening. The poet feels peaceful in the lap of nature.

(*iii*) It is clear that the poet's heart aches to go back to Innisfree. Even amidst the concrete jungle, his heart can hear the sounds coming from the lake.

***Q* 2.** By now you may have concluded that Innisfree is a simple, natural place, full of beauty and peace. How does the poet contrast it with where he now stands? (Read stanza 3)

Ans. 'The Lake Isle of Innisfree' is calm and peaceful place. Unlike the natural surroundings of that place, the city in which the poet lives is made of concrete. The lake is nowhere to be seen and his heart aches to get far away from the roadways and pavements.

***Q*3.** Do you think Innisfree is only a place or a state of mind? Does the poet actually miss the place of his boyhood days?

Ans. Innisfree is both a place and a state of mind. If that had not been so, then we would not have felt the need to get away from the busy city life where there is so much of rush in everything.

The poet surely misses the place of his boyhood days. It gets apparent when he says that even though he is standing on the pavement, he could hear and feel the shore of the lake deep within his heart.

II. ***Q*1.** Look at the words the poet uses to describe what he sees and hears at Innisfree.

(i) Bee-loud glade
(ii) Evenings full of the linnet's wings
(iii) Lake water lapping with low sounds

What pictures do these words create in your mind?

Ans. (*i*) These words bring to our minds the image of buzzing bees.

(*ii*) These words bring-up the image of linnets flying across an evening sky.

(*iii*) These words evoke not only the image, but also the soft sound of a lake's water washing the shore as if one is standing near a lake.

***Q*2.** Look at these words;

.... peace comes dropping slow

Dropping from the veils of the morning to where the cricket sings

What do these words mean to you? What do you think "comes dropping slow...from the veils of the morning"? What does "to where the cricket sings" mean?

Ans. These words represent a peaceful morning scene. The given lines indicate that peace of mind can be slowly acquired from the natural surroundings.

It is peace that "comes dropping slow ... from the veils of the morning".

The phrase "to where the cricket sings" indicates a peaceful place where one can hear the vibrant sounds of the nature-sounds such as the songs of the crickets.

5

A Legend of the Northland

Phoebe Cary

Chapter Sketch

The poem is a story in itself. It teaches us that one should not be selfish. The narrative starts from the typical lines and then takes the reader on a ride. The poetess herself calls it a lesson. Saint Peter was hungry and he asked for some food from a lady. She was selfish and didn't give him any. The Saint grew angry and punished her.

Detailed Summary

Description of Northland

Northland is a place far away. The nights are so long in winter that people can't even sleep through them. The people harness the reindeers to sledges when it snows. The children wear furry clothes and look like baby cubs. A tale is very famous there about a saint. It is more of a lesson.

Saint Peter was Hungry

Saint Peter went about preaching on earth. He came around a house where a woman was baking cakes. He was very hungry. He asked her to give him just a single one from her store of cakes.

The Lady was Selfish

The lady baked a small cake. But she thought that it was too large. She made a smaller one. But thought it was still big. Then she baked one which was thin as a wafer. The selfish lady couldn't part it with either. She puts them on the shelf thinking that her cakes seem small when she eats them, but too large when she was going to give them away.

Saint Peter gets Angry Punishes Her

The saint was very hungry and the selfish woman's behaviour was enough to provoke him. Saint Peter grew angry and punished her. He said that she should not live in human form and cursed her that she should live and eat like a bird. She turned into a woodpecker. All her clothes got burned. Schoolboys still find her boring in the woods.

Exercises

Thinking about the Poem

I. ***Q* 1.** Which country or countries do you think "the Northland" refers to?

Ans. The name of the country *i.e.,* Northland itself suggests that the country is situated near the polar region. Other things that support this view are that the days are short nights are very long there and it even snows. It may refer to Russia or Iceland.

***Q* 2.** What did Saint Peter ask the old lady for? What was the lady's reaction?

Ans. Saint Peter was roaming about on earth, preaching as he was used to. He got very hungry and reached the cottage of the old lady. He asked her to give just one cake. The lady was very selfish. She made a very small cake, but couldn't even part away with it.

***Q* 3.** How did he punish her?

Ans. The old lady's selfish behaviour was enough to provoke the placid Saint. He said that the lady was too selfish to live in human form. He punished her by changing her into a woodpecker to collect her food by boring into the woods.

***Q* 4.** How does the woodpecker get her food?

Ans. The woodpecker has a long and strong beak which it uses to bore into the dry hard woods of trees and collect food.

Q5. Do you think that the old lady would have been so ungenerous if she had known who Saint Peter really was? What would she have done then?

Ans. The lady might have not been so ungenerous if she had known who Saint Peter really was because then she would have feared that the saint might punish her if she behaved in a not so moral way.

Q6. Is this a true story? Which part of this poem do you feel is the most important?

Ans. The story doesn't seem to be true as incantations of turning a person into a bird have no logical reasoning behind them. But it surely gives a nice lesson. The part in which Saint Peter says that the old lady was far too selfish to dwell in human form is the most important.

Q7. What is a legend? Why is this poem called a legend?

Ans. A legend is an old traditional story. The story may or may not be true, but tries to teach us something important. This poem is called a legend because it tells an old story of Northland. This is the story of an old greedy woman who angered Saint. Peter.

Q8. Write the story of 'A Legend of the Northland' in about ten sentences.

Ans. In the biting cold of Northland, Saint Peter went about preaching. One day, he reached a cottage and asked the owner of the house, an old lady to give him a cake to eat. The lady baked a small cake, but thought that it was too big to give away. She baked a still smaller one and had the same thought.

Finally, she baked a cake thin as a wafer, but couldn't part away with it either. The selfish nature of the lady angered the saint Peter. He found her too selfish to be a woman. So out of anger he changed her to a wood peeker. She was often seen in the wood living is the trees and continued boring into hard wood for little food. It was the result of saint Peter curse

II. **Q1.** Let's look at the words at the end of the second and fourth lines, *viz*, 'snows' and 'clothes', 'true' and 'you', 'below' and 'know.' We find that 'snows' rhymes with 'clothes', 'true' rhymes with 'you' and 'below' rhymes with 'know'.

Find more such rhyming words.

Ans. There are many rhyming words in the poem. Some of them are earth and hearth, done and one, lay and away, flat and that, faint and saint, form and warm, food and wood, word and bird, same and flame.

Supplementary Reader

1

The Lost Child

Mulk Raj Anand

Chapter Sketch

A child goes to a fair with his parents. He is happy and excited and wants the sweets and toys displayed there. But his parents don't buy them for him citing different reasons. Despite several warnings he kept lagging behind and unfortunately gets lost in the fair.

Detailed Summary

The Child Lagged Behind

The child was with his parents. The family was going to the spring festival. He noticed the toys on the way. He wanted one of them, but the parents denied his request.

The child then started following the dragonflies. He would chase them till one hovered and then flew away. The parents kept telling him to come with them, but he kept lagging behind. The worms and insects would attract him.

The Child Craved for Many Things

The family grew close to the fair. The child could see many other footpaths full of throngs, converging to the whirlpool of the fair and` felt at once repelled and fascinated by the confusion of the world he was entering.

The boy noticed a sweetmeat seller. His mouth watered at seeing his favourite sweet *burfi*. But he knew that his parents won't allow him to have it saying that he was too greedy and so he moved on.

The child felt irresistibly drawn towards the flower-seller who was selling garlands of *gulmohur*. He kept moving on as he knew that his parents would not heed to this request also saying that they were too cheap.

Next the boy wanted to possess the silken coloured balloons. Again he thought that his request would go vain as the parents would say that he was too old for them. He moved on.

The child then laid his eyes upon the snake charmer. But his parents had forbidden him to hear such coarse music and so, he kept moving on.

The Child Gets Lost

There was a merry-go-round in full swing. Men, women and children, carried away in a whirling motion, shrieked and cried with dizzy laughter. The child watched them intently and then he made a bold request, "I want to go on the merry-go-round, please, Father, Mother".

But there was no reply, with horror he realised that he was alone and his parents were not to be found. A deep cry came from his throat and tears rolled down his eyes. He was panic-stricken. He started running hither and thither. His yellow turban came untied and his clothes became muddy.

A Man Finds the Child

The child ran towards the shrine. A vast multitude was converging there. Every little inch of space was congested with men. He ran through people's legs searching for his parents. The poor child struggled to thrust a way between their feet. He got knocked to and fro by their brutal movements. He might have been trampled underfoot, had he not shrieked at the highest pitch of his voice, "Father, Mother!" A man in the surging crowd heard his cry and stooping with great difficulty, lifted him up in his arms.

He asked about the child's whereabouts. The man tried to comfort him.

All the Things Lose Interest

The man took him to the round about, but the child wanted his parents. He took him to the snake-charmer but the child wailed for his father and mother only. Then the man tried to distract his attention by asking him if he wanted balloons or flower garlands. The child wanted neither. He craved for his parents till now. All the things that he had wanted had lost all his interest.

Exercises

Q1. What are the things the child sees on his way to the fair? Why does he lag behind?

Ans. The child was very fascinated by the things he encountered on the way. Firstly, he ran towards the toys shop. He also ran after the dragonflies. He kept looking at the little insects and worms along the footpath. Hence, he lagged behind.

Q2. In the fair he wants many things. What are they? Why does he move on without waiting for an answer?

Ans. He wants to have his favourite sweet burfi. He then was drawn towards a garland of gulmohur. He also wanted some balloons. He kept moving on as he knew that his parents won't buy these things for him.

Q3. When does he realise that he has lost his way? How have his anxiety and insecurity been described?

Ans. The boy realised that he has been lost when he wanted to ride a round about. He called out for his parent but there was no reply. He began to cry in fear. Tear rolled down his eyes. Panic-stricken, he ran in all directions searching for his parents. His turban got untied and his clothes became muddy.

Q4. Why does the lost child lose interest in the things that he had wanted earlier?

Ans. The boy was happy as he had the company and security of his parents. He had interest in all the things only till he was with them. But after he was lost he wanted to be with his parents only. He was a scared and panic-stricken child. Only his parents could have given him relief after that.

Q5. What do you think happens in the end? Does the child find his parents?

Ans. In the end the boy was found by a man who tried to comfort him. The story after that is quite blurry. I think that the man would have helped the boy search for his parents. There are always 'lost and found' centers present in such fairs. He would have dropped him there.

2

The Adventures of Toto

Ruskin Bond

Chapter Sketch

The narrator's grandfather brings a monkey home, named Toto. He wanted to keep him in his private zoo. Thus, began Toto's adventures. He is a constant nuisance and a trouble maker. The grandfather finally decides that the home is not the right place for him and sells him back.

Detailed Summary

Grandfather Brings Toto Home

The grandfather had pity on Toto when he saw him tied to a feeding-trough. Grandfather decided that he would add the little fellow to his private zoo. He bought Toto from the tonga-driver for a sum of five rupees.

Grandfather Finds Toto Pretty

Toto was a pretty monkey. His bright eyes sparkled with mischief beneath deep-set eyebrows and his teeth, which were a pearly white were very often displayed in a smile that frightened the life out of elderly Anglo-Indian ladies. But his hands looked dried-up as though they had been pickled in the sun for many years. Yet his fingers were quick and wicked and his tail, while adding to his good looks (grandfather believed a tail would add to anyone's good looks), also served as a third hand for Toto. He could use it to hang from a branch and it was capable of scooping up any delicacy that might be out of reach of his hands. Toto's presence was kept a secret as the grandmother always fussed about animals that the grandfather brought home.

The Grandfather Considered Toto Clever

Grandfather and the narrator tied Toto to a peg fastened into the wall of the narrator's room. A few hours later when they returned, they found that the little money had wrenched the peg from the socket, torn off the ornamental wallpaper and shredded the narrator's school blazer. The grandfather was rather amused. He thought that Toto was a clever monkey and he could have escaped after making a rope from the shredded clothes.

The Grandfather Takes Toto to Saharanpur

Toto was transferred to a big cage in the servants' quarters where a number of grandfather's pets lived very sociably together. But the monkey wouldn't allow any of his companions to sleep at night; so grandfather, who had to leave Dehradun next day to collect his pension in Saharanpur, decided to take him along.

A big black canvas kit-bag was provided for Toto. When the bag was closed, there was no escape. Toto could not get his hands through the opening and the canvas was not too strong for him to bite his way through. His efforts to get out only had the effect of making the bag roll about on the floor or occasionally jump into the air—an exhibition that attracted a curious crowd of onlookers on the Dehradun railway platform.

The Ticket-Collector Calls Toto a Dog

Toto managed to get his head out at the instant when the grandfather was producing his ticket to the ticket-collector. The ticket-collector considered him to be a dog. The grandfather tried to explain to him that Toto was not a dog, not even a quadruped but the ticket-collector was adamant. He charged the grandfather three rupees as his fair.

Toto—A Nuisance

Toto was finally accepted by the grandmother and he was given a comfortable home in the stable. The family donkey, Nana, was his companion there. On Toto's first night in the stable, grandfather paid him a visit. To his surprise he found Nana, without apparent cause, pulling at her halter and trying to keep her head as far as possible from a bundle of hay. Grandfather discovered that Toto was fastened on to her long ears with his sharp little teeth. Toto and Nana never became friends.

Toto Learned to Bathe

Toto had learned to bathe by aping the narrator. The large bowl of warm water for his bath was a treat for him in cold winter evenings. He would carefully test the temperature of the bath with his hand, apply soap and then rub around his whole body. After the water got cold he would rush to the kitchen-fire to dry himself.

Toto Nearly Boils Himself

One day, a large kitchen kettle had been left on the fire to boil for tea and Toto decided to remove the lid. Finding the water just warm enough for a bath Toto stepped in. The water began to boil. Toto then raised himself a little; but, finding it cold outside, sat down again. He continued hopping up and down for some time, until grandmother arrived and pulled him, half-boiled, out of the kettle.

Not the Sort of Pet they could Keep for Long

One day, a dish of *pullao* was prepared by the grandmother. When the family entered the room, they found Toto stuffing himself with rice. The grandmother screamed and Toto threw a plate at her. One of the narrator's aunts rushed forward and received a glass of water in the face. When grandfather arrived, Toto picked up the dish of *pullao* and made his exit through a window. He climbed up the jackfruit tree. He remained there all afternoon, determined on finishing every grain. And then, in order to spite grandmother, who had screamed at him, he threw the dish down from the tree and chattered with delight when it broke into a hundred pieces.

Obviously, Toto was not the sort of pet they could keep for long. They were not well-to-do and could not afford the frequent loss of dishes, clothes, curtains and wallpaper. So grandfather sold Toto back to the tonga-driver for only three rupees.

Exercises

Q1. How does Toto come to the grandfather's private zoo?

Ans. Grandfather bought Toto from a tonga-driver for the sum of five rupees. The tonga-driver used to keep Toto tied to a feeding-trough. The grandfather had pity on him and bought the little red monkey for his private zoo.

Q2. "Toto was a pretty monkey." In what sense is Toto pretty?

Ans. Toto was a pretty monkey. Mischief sparkled in his deep-set eyes. He also had pearly white teeth. Though his smile scared the wits out of elderly Anglo-Indian ladies. He had quick and wicked hands. The grandfather thought that the long tail added to his good looks.

Q3. Why does grandfather take Toto to Saharanpur and how? Why does the ticket-collector insist on calling Toto a dog?

Ans. The grandfather decided to take Toto to Saharanpur as he didn't let other animals sleep. A big black canvas kit-bag was provided for Toto. The ticket-collector classified Toto as a dog as he had four legs.

Q4. How does Toto take a bath? Where has he learnt to do this? How does Toto almost boil himself alive?

Ans. Toto has learned to bath by aping the narrator. He tests the temperature of the water and then steps into it for the bath. Once, water was kept in a kettle to boil for tea. Toto got into it. He kept jumping up and down as the water boiled. He was pulled by the grandmother as half-boiled.

Q5. Why does the author say, "Toto was not the sort of pet we could keep for long"?

Ans. The narrator's family was not very rich. They could not afford the frequent loss of dishes, clothes, curtains and wallpapers. He was quite a nuisance around the house. So, the grandfather sold him back to the tonga-driver for only three rupees.

3

Iswaran the Storyteller

R.K. Laxman

Chapter Sketch

The story revolves around a domestic help, Iswaran. He is a very good storyteller. His stories are always filled with mystery and his valiant efforts. His boss, Mahendra, considered him an asset. One day, Iswaran tells Mahendra about a ghost. Mahendra rubbishes his story but encounters something obscure. He decides to leave the haunted place the very next day.

Detailed Summary

Mahendra

The story was narrated to Ganesh by a young man, Mahendra, who was a juniour supervisor in a firm. Mahendra's job was to keep an eye on the activities at the work site. He had to keep moving from place to place every now and then as ordered by his head office.

Iswaran—An Asset to Mahendra

Mahendra was a bachelor. His needs were simple and he was able to adjust himself to all kinds of odd conditions. But one asset he had was his cook, Iswaran. The cook was quite attached to Mahendra and followed him uncomplainingly wherever he was posted. He cooked for Mahendra, washed his clothes and chatted away with his master at night. He could weave out endless stories and anecdotes on varied subjects.

Iswaran also had an amazing capacity to produce vegetables and cooking ingredients, seemingly out of nowhere. He would miraculously conjure up the most delicious dishes made with fresh vegetables within an hour of arriving at the new workplace.

The Exaggerated Stories of Iswaran

Iswaran's descriptions were greatly influenced by the Tamil authors that he read. When he was narrating even the smallest of incidents, he would try to work in suspense and a surprise ending into the account. For example, instead of saying that he had come across an uprooted tree on the highway, he would say, with eyebrows suitably arched and hands held out in a dramatic gesture, "The road was deserted and I was all alone. Suddenly I spotted something that looked like an enormous bushy beast lying sprawled across the road. I was half inclined to turn and go back. But as I came closer I saw that it was a fallen tree, with its dry branches spread out". Mahendra was completely absorbed in his stories.

One of the other stories involved Iswaran taming an angry Elephant just by a stick. He claimed that he had learned the ancient art of karate or ju-jitsu. He had a knack of telling stories. He knew how to keep his listener interested and when to leave them hanging for more. Whether the story was credible or not, Mahendra enjoyed listening to it because of the inimitable way in which it was told.

Mahendra didn't Believe in Ghosts

One day, Iswaran told Mahendra that the entire factory area was once a burial ground. He also said that he encountered human skulls and bones every now and then. He then narrated an incident in which he saw a ghost holding a foetus in her hands. But Mahendra didn't seem to believe his story. He called Iswaran crazy and also that there is nothing like ghosts and spirits.

From that day Mahendra slept rather uneasily. He avoided looking out of his window altogether when the moon was full.

The Obscure Experience

One night, Mahendra was woken up from his sleep by a low moan close to his window. At first he thought that it was a cat. He resisted looking outside. But the wailing became louder and less feline. Mustering up some courage, he looked out at the white sheet of moonlight outside. There, not too far away, was a dark cloudy form clutching a bundle. Mahendra broke into a cold sweat and fell back on the pillow, panting.

As he gradually recovered from the ghastly experience he began to reason with himself and finally concluded that it must have been some sort of trick that his subconscious had played on him.

Mahendra Decided to Leave the Place

The next morning, just as Mahendra was stepping out Iswaran grinned and said that Mahendra had himself witnessed the female ghost last night. He knew because he had heard wailing sounds coming from Mahendra's room. A chill went down Mahendra's spine. He did not wait for Iswaran to complete his sentence. He hurried away to his office and handed in his papers, resolving to leave the haunted place the very next day!

Exercises

***Q*1.** In what way is Iswaran an asset to Mahendra?

Ans. Iswaran is certainly an asset to Mahendra. He is his cook, his laundryman, a constant company in the house. Moreover, Iswaran is quite entertaining. He keeps telling Mahendra interesting stories.

***Q*2.** How does Iswaran describe the uprooted tree on the highway? What effect does he want to create in his listeners?

Ans. Iswaran's stories were an exaggerated version of the reality. He would say that a bushy beast was sprawled across the road. He coupled it with arched eyebrows and hand gestures. He wants to create suspense and surprise.

***Q*3.** How does he narrate the story of the tusker? Does it appear to be plausible?

Ans. He narrates the story with total drama and exaggeration. He was a young kid then and stunned the mad beast with only a stick. No, he doesn't appear to be plausible as the act that he describes has deep loopholes in it.

Q4. Why does the author say that Iswaran seemed to more than make up for the absence of a TV in Mahendra's living quarters?

Ans. Iswaran was a constant rant. Not a single day passed without his narration. Every story was packed with adventure, horror and suspense. Mahendra enjoyed all his stories. He would hear them with rapt attention. Thus, he never needed a TV.

Q5. Mahendra calls ghosts or spirits a figment of the imagination. What happens to him on a full-moon night?

Ans. Mahendra doesn't seem to believe Iswaran stories about ghosts. They are a figment of imagination to him. But one full-moon night, he himself encountered a ghost of a sort. The ghost was some cloudy form holding a bundle. His heart skipped a beat and he kept panting.

Q6. Can you think of some other ending for the story?

Ans. The story could have ended differently. After the ghostly experience, Mahendra decides to prove Iswaran wrong. He sets-up a trap for the ghost and finds that the ghost was actually none other than Iswaran himself.

4

In the Kingdom of Fools

A Kannada Folktale

Chapter Sketch

The humorous story is an apt depiction of how foolishness can be harmful to us and others around us. Moreover, it can have dangerous consequences if the rulers and lawmakers are foolish.

A guru and his disciple reach a kingdom of fools. The guru decides to leave but the disciple, palled with the ignorance and money-mindedness, stays behind. Circumstances force him to regret his decision when the foolish king tries to execute him even when he has not committed any mistake.

Detailed Summary

The Guru and the Disciple Arrive in the Kingdom of Fools

In the kingdom of fools, both the king and the minister were idiots. They didn't want to run things like other kings, so they decided to change night into day and day into night. They ordered that everyone should be awake at night and work only after dark and go to bed as soon as the sun came up. Anyone who disobeyed would be punished with death. The people did as they were told for fear of death.

One day a guru and his disciple arrived in the city. It was a beautiful city, it was broad daylight, but there was no one about. Even the cattle had been taught to sleep by day. The two strangers were amazed by what they saw around them and wandered around town till the evening, when suddenly the whole town woke up and went about its 'nightly' business.

Everything Cost One *Duddu*

The guru and the disciple were astonished to find that everything cost the same, a single *duddu*-whether they bought a measure of rice or a bunch of bananas, it cost a *duddu*. The guru and his disciple were delighted. They had never heard of anything like this. They could buy all the food they wanted for a rupee.

The guru realised that it was a kingdom of fools. He told his disciple that the place was not meant for them and they should leave immediately. The disciple was reluctant. Everything was so cheap. The guru said that the fools cannot be trusted. They can never tell what will happen next.

The guru gave in and left. The disciple stayed back. He ate like anything and grew very fat.

The Fool's Justice

One bright day, a thief broke into a rich merchant's house. He had made a hole in the wall and sneaked in and as he was carrying out his loot, the wall of the old house collapsed on his head and killed him on the spot. His brother ran to the king and complained that his brother was pursuing his 'ancient trade' when the wall fell on him and killed him. He said that it was the merchant's mistake who hadn't built a strong wall.

The king at once summoned the owner of the house. He accused the merchant of killing the thief and said that he would be punished.

The Merchant's Plea

The merchant pleaded that it was not him who had the wall built. The wall was built in his father's time and so the man who built it was to be blamed for the weak construction. He blamed the bricklayer for the fault. The bricklayer was summoned.

The Bricklayer's Excuse

The bricklayer admitted that the wall built by him was no good. But that was because his mind was not on it. He remembered very well a dancing girl who was going up and down that street all day with her anklets jingling and he couldn't keep his eyes or his mind on his work. And so, the dancing girl, now an old woman, came trembling to the court.

The Case Deepens

The old lady argued that though she was the girl who had distracted the bricklayer but it was no fault of his. She said that she had given some gold to make jewellery to the goldsmith. The goldsmith was very lazy. He gave her many excuses and made her run up and down all day. The king thought that the old lady was not to be blamed. The real culprit was the goldsmith.

The Buck Keeps Passing On

The goldsmith had his own story. He said that it was true that he had made many excuses to the girl but it was only because the merchant's had a wedding and they wanted their jewellery first. They were so impatient that the goldsmith had to complete their work first. The merchant was none other than the original owner of the house. The merchant tried to reason with the king saying that it was his father who had ordered the jewellery.

The King's Justice

His requests went unheard as the king and his minister decided that the merchant had inherited everything from his father. The king claimed that he could see through his eyes that he was a sinner and so he must be executed.

The Disciple Gets Entangled in the Mess

It occurred to the merchant and the king that the merchant was too thin to be properly executed at the new stake. It struck to them that they needed to find a person who was fat and enough to fit the stake. The servants went searching and their eye fell on the disciple who had fattened himself for months. The disciple cried that he was innocent but it was the royal decree that they must execute a person who would fit the stake.

The Wise Guru

The disciple now remembered his guru's advice. The guru arrived to save him. He told the king that he should be executed first and then his disciple. The king demanded that why the wise man wanted to be killed. The guru explained to him that the stake was the god of justice, it was new. The first person to be executed on it will reborn as king of the country in his next life and the person executed next would become his minister.

The king didn't want to lose his kingdom even in the next life. He postponed the execution.

The New King and The Minister

The king consulted with his minister and decided that they should be the ones to die on the stake. The king ordered the executioners to kill the guru and the disciple when they come to them at night.

That night they released the guru and the disciple, disguised themselves as the two and went to the executioners. People panicked when they saw that it was the body of the king and the minister. They mourned and discussed the future of their country. They went to the guru and his disciple. They wanted to make them their new king and minister. They accepted the proposal. After that they everything went to normal.

Exercises

Q1. What are the two strange things the guru and his disciple find in the kingdom of fools?

Ans. The guru and his disciple found that all people were asleep in the broad daylight. Shops were closed and there was no one in the streets. Even the cattle were trained to sleep by the day. Secondly, there was everything very cheap and cost the same, a single *duddu*.

Q2. Why does the disciple decide to stay in the kingdom of fools? Is it a good idea?

Ans. Everything was cheap and cost the same, a single *duddu*, in the kingdom of fools. The guru was a wise man. He feared the worse and decided to leave the place immediately. But the disciple was tempted to stay to feed on delicious food that was available so cheaply.

Q3. Name all the people who are tried in the king's court and give the reasons for their trial.

Ans. The first one to be tried was the owner of the house. He was tried for building the weak wall. The second was the bricklayer who had built the wall. Then a dancing girl was blamed for distracting the mason. And then the goldsmith who was accused of making the dancing girl walk by delaying her jewellery and the last one was the rich man who had ordered the jewellery.

Q4. **Who is the real culprit according to the king? Why does he escape punishment?**

Ans. The real culprit, according to the king was the original owner of the house *i.e.,* the merchant. He tried to save himself by saying that his father was the actual owner. But it was all vain.

He escaped the punishment because the king thought that he was too thin for the stake.

Q5. **What are the guru's words of wisdom? When does the disciple remember them?**

Ans. The guru was an insightful person who realised that there can be no justice in the kingdom of fools. He had warned his disciple that it was a kingdom of fools and he could never tell what they would do next. He also suggested that they should leave the kingdom immediately.

The disciple remembered these words when he was found fit to be put on stake.

Q6. **How does the guru manage to save his disciple's life?**

Ans. The guru was very intelligent and he had many magic powers to see the past and the future. He tricked the king into believing that the first person to die on the new stake would become the king of the kingdom in the next life. The second to die would become the minister. The king and the minister didn't want to lose the kingdom in the next life also and so they got themselves executed.

5

The Happy Prince

Oscar Wilde

Chapter Sketch

The Happy Prince is a story of sacrifice and kindness. The Happy Prince never knew suffering until he died and his statue was mounted on a high place. From there, he could see all the pain in his kingdom. He wanted to help his people. Just then a swallow arrived. He requested the swallow to help him. Though the swallow wanted to go to Egypt, he stayed back and helped the prince. They gave their all to help others and the swallow died in the process.

Detailed Summary

The Swallow Meets the Happy Prince

High above the city, on a tall column, stood the statue of the Happy Prince. He was gilded all over with thin leaves of fine gold, for eyes he had two bright sapphires and a large red ruby glowed on his sword hilt.

One night, a little swallow flew over the city. His friends had gone away to Egypt six weeks before, but he had stayed behind; then he decided to go to Egypt too.

He was searching for a shelter when he saw the statue on the tall column. He alighted just between the feet of the Happy Prince. When he was about to sleep rain drops started to fall on him, but there was no rain. He noticed that they were actually tears. The Happy Prince's statue was crying.

The Happy Prince is Sad

The swallow asked the prince that why was he crying. The prince replied that when he was alive he never knew sadness. His courtiers called him the Happy Prince and happy indeed he was. But after his death, his statue was mounted on a high place from where he could witness all the pain and suffering in his kingdom.

The Prince Requests the Swallow to Help him

The prince told the swallow that from the pedestal he could see a woman seated at a table. She was a seamstress. She was embroidering flowers on a satin gown. In a bed in the corner of the room her little boy was lying ill. He had a fever and was asking his mother to give him oranges. His mother had nothing to give him but river water, so he was crying. He asked the swallow to take the ruby from his sword hilt and give it to the poor seamstress. The swallow denied the request at first as he wanted to go to Egypt but then gave in seeing the sad face of the prince. Thus, he took the ruby and flew to the house of the seamstress. He laid the ruby on the table and before leaving fanned the boy's head.

After he returned to the prince, he said that he felt warm even though it was cold. The prince explained to him that it was because he had done a good deed.

Helping the Playwright

The Happy Prince asks the swallow to stay for one more night. He sent the swallow to a playwright who was feeling too cold and hungry to write. The prince asked the swallow to pluck one sapphire from his eye and give it to the poor playwright. The playwright was happy. The swallow returned and told the prince that he was leaving but the prince asks him to stay for one more night.

Helping the Matchgirl

The Happy Prince told the swallow that there was a little matchgirl whose all matches had fallen into the gutter. Her father would beat her if she didn't bring home some money. The prince asked the swallow to pluck another sapphire from his eye and give it to her. The swallow did as the prince had asked.

The Swallow doesn't go to Egypt

The prince was blind now. The swallow decided to live with him. He told him marvellous stories of distant lands. The prince said that the most marvellous thing was the suffering of humans. "There is no Mystery so great as Misery", said he.

Helping the Others

The swallow flew over the city and reported what he saw. He saw that the rich were making merrier and the beggars were suffering. He also saw the white faces of starving children. The prince asked the swallow to take the leaf after leaf of the fine gold over his body and give it to the poor. The swallow did the thing as the prince requested him to.

The Swallow Dies

The winter set in. It was bitter cold. But the swallow didn't leave the prince. He knew his last had come. He told the prince that he was going. The prince said that he was happy that the swallow was finally going to Egypt. It was not so. The swallow died there after kissing the prince on his lips.

The not-so-Happy Prince

The moment the swallow died, there appeared a crack in the lead heart of the prince. The next day, the mayor and his councilors decided that the prince didn't look better than a beggar and he should be removed. They also saw the dead swallow at his feet.

Two Most Precious Things

The prince's statue was melted but his lead heart would not melt. They threw it away. God asked one of the angels to bring the two most precious things from the city. The angel brought the leaden heart and the dead swallow. God agreed that those things were the most precious.

Exercises

Q1. Why do the courtiers call the prince 'The Happy Prince'? Is he really happy? What does he see all around him?

Ans. The courtiers called the prince 'the Happy Prince' because he was indeed happy. He never knew sorrow in his lifetime. Sorrow was miles away from his palace. But he was not happy at the present. His statue was mounted on a high place and from there he could see all the sadness and suffering in his kingdom.

Q 2. Why does the Happy Prince send a ruby for the seamstress? What does the swallow do in the seamstress' house?

Ans. The seamstress little boy was ill. He wanted to have oranges. But they were very poor. The mother was unable to give him oranges. The Happy Prince wanted to help them and thus sent a ruby for the seamstress.

The swallow laid down the ruby on the table but before leaving he gently fanned the boy's forehead.

Q3. For whom does the prince send the sapphires and why?

Ans. The Prince's eyes were made of sapphires. He sent one of them to a young playwright. The playwright was trying to finish a play but it was bitter cold and there was no fire in his grate. Moreover, he was fainting because of hunger.

The second sapphire was meant for a matchgirl who was crying because all her matches fell into the gutter. She feared scolding because if she not take some money at home then her father beat her.

Q4. What does the swallow see when it flies over the city?

Ans. The swallow flew over the city and saw the atrocities of the world. He saw that rich men enjoying life in their beautiful homes and beggars were sitting at the gates. Then he saw hungry children with white faces. He also saw guards turning two boys away. He saw numerous sufferings.

Q5. Why did the swallow not leave the prince and go to Egypt?

Ans. The swallow desperately wanted to go to Egypt where all his friends were. At first, he waited at the request of the prince. He helped him in his all subjects. Thereafter when the prince went blind, as he gifted both the sapphires, the swallow didn't want to leave the blind prince behind.

Q6. What are the precious things mentioned in the story? Why are they precious?

Ans. The two precious things mentioned in the story are not the riches and jewels. But they are the heart of the Happy Prince and the dead swallow. They are precious because they are epitomes of kindness and sacrifice. They understood the misery of the others.

Term II

Packing

Jerome K. Jerome

Chapter Sketch

The chapter is taken from the narrator's novel "Three Men in a Boat". Here he narrates a humorous incident which happened when they were packing for the road trip.

Detailed Summary

The Narrator Decides to Pack

The narrator was proud of his packing skills. Thus, he decided to pack when the three friends decided to go on a boat trip. But actually by pack he meant that he loved to head the task. His friends George and Harris relaxed as he was packing and this irritated the narrator. He hated seeing people doing nothing when he was working.

The Narrator Gets Hysteric While Packing

When the narrator finished packing, Harris told him that he had forgotten to put the boots in. When he packed his boots and strapped the bags, he realised that he couldn't recall if he had packed his toothbrush. He always used to forget his toothbrush. He turned everything out and finally found the brush. He packed his tobacco pouch by mistake and hence had to repack it again.

More Hysteria

Harris and George were certainly not good at packing. The created a mess. Many things were spoiled and many were broken. But the narrator didn't try to help them. This irritated George and Harris. They couldn't find things, lost the butter, broke things and squashed others.

Montmorency Joins the Show

The narrator says that it was Montmorency's ambition to get scolded. He had the knack of creating trouble. He sat down on things and disturbed them while they were on the task. He 'killed' lemons. Finally Harris chased him away with a frying pan.

The Group gets Tired

The friends were tired after packing. All they wanted to do was sleep. But that was not it. They slept only after having a tussle over the time they should wake up.

Exercises

Thinking about the Text

I. *Discuss in pairs and answer each question below in a short paragraph (30-40 words).*

Q 1. How many characters are there in the narrative? Name them. (Don't forget the dog!).

Ans. There are four characters in the narrative. They are the narrator himself Jerome, George, Harris and the dog named Montmorency.

Q 2. Why did the narrator (Jerome) volunteer to do the packing?

Ans. The narrator volunteered to do the packing because he was proud of his packing skills. According to him, it was one of those things which he knew more about than any other person living. But as it turned out, it was not very correct.

Q 3. How did George and Harris react to this? Did Jerome like their reaction?

Ans. George and Harris at once accepted Jerome's suggestion. George put on a pipe and spread himself over the easy-chair and Harris cocked his legs on the table and lit a cigar. Jerome didn't like it. He was irritated.

Q 4. What was Jerome's real intention when he offered to pack?

Ans. When Jerome had made the suggestion that he would pack, he actually intended that he would boss the job. He would supervise Harris and George in the packing. He would push them aside every now and then, teach them how to do the packing properly.

Q 5. What did Harris say after the bag was shut and strapped? Why do you think he waited till then to ask?

Ans. After the bag was shut and strapped, Harris asked Jerome, if he had put the boots in. It seems that it was his habit not to say a word until the job was finished. He wouldn't have said a word until he had shut and strapped the bag.

Q 6. What "horrible idea" occurred to Jerome a little later?

Ans. After Jerome was done with packing a "horrible idea" occurred to him. The horrible idea was if he had packed his toothbrush or not. He always forgot if he had packed his toothbrush or not.

Q 7. Where did Jerome finally find the toothbrush?

Ans. Jerome turned the bag upside down to find his toothbrush. After going through everything he had packed and futile searching, Jerome finally found the toothbrush inside a boot.

Q 8. Why did Jerome have to reopen the packed bag?

Ans. Jerome packed the bag after finding his toothbrush. But unfortunately, he had packed his tobacco pouch in it. He had to reopen the bag to take it out.

Q 9. What did George and Harris offer to pack and why?

Ans. George and Harris offered to pack the hampers for carrying food as they weren't packed yet. They had to start in less than twelve hours and the packing was still left. They wanted to save their time.

Q 10. While packing the hamper, George and Harris do a number of foolish and funny things.

Tick the statements that are true.

(*i*) They started with breaking a cup.

(*ii*) They also broke a plate.

(*iii*) They squashed a tomato.

(*iv*) They trod on the butter.

(*v*) They stepped on a banana.

(*vi*) They put things behind them and couldn't find them.

(*vii*) They stepped on things.

(*viii*) They packed the pictures at the bottom and put heavy things on top.

(*ix*) They upset almost everything.

(x) They were very good at packing.

Ans. Statements i, iii, iv, vi, vii and ix are true.

II. ***Q* 1.** What does Jerome say was Montmorency's ambition in life? What do you think of Montmorency and why?

Ans. According to Jerome, Montmorency's ambition in life is to get in the way and get scolded. He would always be present at a place where he wasn't wanted, be a perfect nuisance and make people mad. He enjoyed things thrown at its head. His day is not completed without all these activities. His highest aim and object in his life was to get somebody to stumble over him and curse hit steadily for an hour.

He was surly a nuisance. He created a ruckus when George and Harris were packing. He "killed" three lemons. But the narrator feels that Montmorency cannot be blamed for all this. It is because of the natural, original sin that is born in him.

III. *Discuss in groups and answer the following questions in two or three paragraphs (100-150 words).*

***Q* 1.** Of the three, Jerome, George and Harris, who do you think is the best or worst packer? Support your answer with details from the text.

Ans. In my opinion, all three friends, Jerome, George and Harris prove to be bad at packing things. But Jerome seems to be a bit less worse than the other two. Jerome thought that he had a knack of packing things and he took pride in his skill. However, his packing skills are not very good. He forgot to pack the boots. He himself said that he could not remember if he had packed his toothbrush or not. Finally when he is done with the packing, he realises that he has accidentally packed his tobacco-pouch. He kept packing and unpacking the bag.

George and Harris proved to be a lot worse than Jerome. They totally created a mess. They broke a cup; packed heavy things on top of light items; put things behind them and then couldn't find them when they wanted them; stepped on things; and upset almost everything.

Q 2. How did Montmorency 'contribute' to the packing?

Ans. Montmorency "contributed" in the packing by creating a ruckus. It was his ambition to come into people's ways and be cursed. He always tried to be the perfect nuisance. He actually liked it when people got mad at him man threw stuff at his head. His day was wasted if somebody didn't stumble over him and give him an earful for an hour.

However, Jerome said that Montmorency did not require any encouragement. He had a natural and original sin that he was born with. He came and sat down on things just when they were about to be packed. Whenever Harris or George reached out their hand for anything, it was his cold damp nose their hands met. He put its leg into the jam and disturbed the teaspoons. He went into the hamper and "killed" three lemons.

Q 3. Do you find this story funny? What are the humorous elements in it?

(Pick out at least three, think about what happens, as well as how it is described.)

Ans. The story is indeed a humorous one. The way three grownups, accompanied by a dog, make a fool out of themselves is really hilarious. The fun begins from the start when is misunderstood by his friends, when he says that he wants to do the packing. Next, the narrator claims that he has a knack for packing. The way he unpacks and repacks the same things three times surly tickles the funny bone.

His friends are far worse than him. They create a total mess. They broke things and sat on them then tried to find them. Things get funnier when Montmorency decides to play his part. The narrator describes how Montmorency pretended that lemons were rats and got into the hamper and "killed" three before Harris could land a frying pan on him.

Thinking about Language

I. *Match the words/phrases in Column A with their meanings in Column B.*

A		B	
1.	Slaving	(i)	A quarrel or an argument
2.	Chaos	(ii)	Remove something from inside another thing using a sharp tool
3.	Rummage	(iii)	Strange, mysterious, difficult to explain
4.	Scrape out	(iv)	Finish successfully, achieve
5.	Stumble over, tumble into	(v)	Search for something by moving things around hurriedly or carelessly
6.	Accomplish	(vi)	Complete confusion and disorder
7.	Uncanny	(vii)	Fall or step awkwardly while walking
8.	(To have or get into) A row	(viii)	Working hard

Ans.

A		B	
1.	Slaving	(viii)	Working hard
2.	Chaos	(vi)	Complete confusion and disorder
3.	Rummage	(v)	Search for something by moving things around hurriedly or carelessly
4.	Scrape out	(ii)	Remove something from inside another thing using a sharp tool
5.	Stumble over, tumble into	(vii)	Fall or step awkwardly while walking
6.	Accomplish	(iv)	Finish successfully, achieve
7.	Uncanny	(iii)	Strange, mysterious, difficult to explain
8.	(To have or get into) A row	(i)	A quarrel or an argument

II. *Use suitable words or phrases from Column A to complete the paragraph given below.*

A Traffic Jam

During power cuts, when traffic lights go off, there is utter __________ at crossroads. Drivers add to the confusion by __________ over their right of way and nearly come to blows. Sometimes passers-by, seeing a few policemen __________ at regulating traffic, step in to help. This gives them a feeling of having __________ something.

Ans. During power cuts, when traffic lights go off, there is utter chaos at crossroads. Drivers add to the confusion by getting into a row over their right of way and nearly come to blows. Sometimes passers-by, seeing a few policemen slaving at regulating traffic, step in to help. This gives them a feeling of having accomplished something.

III. *The table below has some proverbs telling you what to do and what not to do. Fill in the blanks and add a few more such proverbs to the table.*

Positive	Negative
(i) *Save* for a rainy day.	(i) *Don't cry* over spilt milk.
(ii) *Make hay* while the sun shines.	(ii) *Don't put* the cart before the horse.
(iii) ______ before yor leap.	(iii) ______ a mountain out of a mole hill.
(iv) ______ and let live.	(iv) ______ all your eggs in one basket.

Ans.

Positive	Negative
(i) *Save* for a rainy day.	(i) *Don't cry* over spilt milk.
(ii) *Make* hay while the sun shines.	(ii) *Don't put* the cart before the horse.
(iii) *Look* before you leap.	(iii) *Don't make* a mountain out of a mole hill.
(iv) *Live* and let live.	(iv) *Don't put* all your eggs in one basket.
(v) *A good beginning* makes a good ending.	(v) *Don't bite* the hand that feeds you.
(vi) *A journey* of a thousand miles begins with a single step.	(vi) *Don't burn* your bridges behind you.
(vii) *A problem* shared is a problem halved.	(vii) *Don't try* to walk before you can crawl.

8

Reach for the Top

Chapter Sketch

The two part chapter contains magnificent feats by two women. Santosh- who conquered Mount Everest and Maria Sharapova- who is a renowned Tennis player. The chapter is the story of their respective journeys and hurdles.

Part I

Detailed Summary

Santosh's Family Background and Birth

Santosh was born in a society where the girl child was not welcomed much. Despite of this she is the only woman who has climbed the Mount Everest twice. A holy man was about to give Santosh's mother the blessing of a son but her grandmother insisted that they wanted a daughter.

Rebel Since Childhood

While the other girls of the village wore traditional Indian clothes, Santosh wore shorts. She was determined to break the social barriers. This was ascertained when she attained the age of sixteen. Her parents wanted her to marry but Santosh wanted to study.

Santosh's Education

Santosh went to a school in Delhi against her parent's wishes. Then she went to Jaipur for higher studies. Her hostel, Kasturba Hostel, was located near the Aravalli Hills. She had the habit of watching the villagers go up the hill and then disappear.

Her Mountaineering Dreams

She decided to check the reason of their disappearing. This was the moment she was encouraged to take up climbing. She saved money. Enrolled herself in Uttarkashi's Nehru Institute of Mountaineering and then there was no looking back. She went straight towards her institute and apologised to her father for taking admission there.

A Remarkable Climber

Thereafter, Santosh went on an expedition every year. Her determination and hard work started bearing fruit. She conquered Mt. Everest in the year 1992. She was twenty then. She was the youngest woman to achieve this feat. She also saved the life of a fellow climber, Mohan Singh. Within twelve months, Santosh found herself a member of an Indo-Nepalese Women's Expedition that invited her to join them. She then scaled the Everest a second time, thus setting a record as the only woman to have scaled the Everest twice.

A Fervent Environmentalist

Santosh says that the experience of hoisting the tricolor on the roof of the world is an indescribable feeling. She was honoured with the Padamashri award. It was truly a spiritual moment. She felt proud as an Indian. Also a fervent environmentalist, Santosh collected and brought down 500 kilograms of garbage from the Himalayas.

Thinking about the Text

I. *Answer these questions in one or two sentences each. (The paragraph numbers within brackets provide clues to the answers.)*

Q 1. Why was the 'holy man' who gave Santosh's mother his blessings surprised? (1)

Ans. The 'holy man' was surprised because Santosh's grandmother told him that they did not want a son.

***Q* 2.** Give an example to show that even as a young girl Santosh was not ready to accept anything unreasonable. (2)

Ans. Where other girls wore traditional Indian dresses, Santosh preferred shorts.

***Q* 3.** Why was Santosh sent to the local school? (3)

Ans. She was sent to the local village school due to the prevailing custom in the family.

***Q* 4.** When did she leave home for Delhi and why? (4)

Ans. When Santosh turned sixteen, her wanted he to get married. Santosh threatened her parents that she would never marry if she did not get a proper education. Therefore, she left home to study in a school in Delhi.

***Q* 5.** Why did Santosh's parents agree to pay for her schooling in Delhi? What mental qualities of Santosh are brought into light by this incident? (4)

Ans. Santosh's parents refused to pay for her education. She informed them that she would earn money by working part time and pay her school fees. Then, her parents agreed to pay for her schooling in Delhi. This shows that Santosh was determined.

II. *Answer each of these questions in a short paragraph (about 30 words).*

***Q* 1.** How did Santosh begin to climb mountains?

Ans. When Santosh was in Jaipur, she watched people from her room in Kasturba Hostel going up the Aravalli Hills and vanishing after a while. She was curious. She went there and found certain mountaineers. They encouraged her to take up climbing. This was how she began climbing mountains.

***Q* 2.** What incidents during the Everest expedition show Santosh's concern for her team-mates?

Ans. During the Everest mission, Santosh helped a dying climber, but she was unsuccessful in saving him. Another climber, Mohan Singh, would surely have died if Santosh hadn't shared her oxygen with him. These incidents show her concern for her team-mates.

***Q* 3.** What shows her concern for the environment?

Ans. Santosh was a fervent environmentalist. While on the Everest mission, she collected and brought down 500 kilograms of garbage from the Himalayas.

***Q* 4.** How does she describe her feelings at the summit of the Everest?

Ans. Santosh says that the feeling at the summit of the Everest was indescribable and it took some moments to sink in. Hoisting the Indian flag was a spiritual moment for her. She felt proud as an Indian.

***Q* 5.** Santosh Yadav got into the record books both times she scaled Mt Everest. What were the reasons for this?

Ans. When Santosh Yadav first scaled Mt Everest, she became the youngest woman in the world to achieve the feat. The second time, she became the only woman to have conquered the Everest twice.

III. *Complete the following statements.*

***Q* 1.** From her room in Kasturba Hostel, Santosh used to ________

Ans. From her room in Kasturba Hostel, Santosh used to *watch villagers going up the hill and suddenly vanishing after a while*.

***Q* 2.** When she finished college, Santosh had to write a letter of apology to her father because ________

Ans. When she finished college, Santosh had to write a letter of apology to her father because *she had got herself enrolled at Uttarkashi's Nehru Institute of Mountaineering without his permission*.

***Q* 3.** During the Everest expedition, her seniors in the team admired her ________ while ________ endeared her to fellow climbers.

Ans. During the Everest expedition, her *seniors in the team admired her climbing skills, physical fitness and mental strength* while *her concern for others and desire to work together with them endeared her to fellow climbers*.

IV. *Pick out words from the text that mean the same as the following words or expressions. (Look in the paragraphs indicated.)*

Q 1. Took to be true without proof (1) ________

Ans. Assumed

Q 2. based on reason; sensible; reasonable (2) ________

Ans. Rational

Q 3. The usual way of doing things (3) ________

Ans. Custom

Q 4. A strong desire arising from within (5) ________

Ans. Urge

Q 5. The power to endure, without falling ill (7) ________

Ans. Resistance

Part II

Maria on Top of the World

Maria attained the number one position in woman's tennis on 22 August 2005. It took four years for the Siberian teenager to achieve her dream. The journey had started nine years ago when she was sent to America at the age of ten to train. She was separated from her mother for about two years. That was a time of struggle. Her father could only earn so much that he could provide for hr training.

Tough Times Made Her Strong

As she was young the others athletes bullied her to tidy up the room and clean it. The tough times made her strong and she got determined and mentally tough. She knew what she wanted. She put aside all the humiliations to pursue her dreams. Her mantra for success is work hard to fulfill your desires.

A Patriot at Heart

Maria accepts that US was a big part of her life but Russia flows in her blood. She is a Russian at heart. She dreams of playing in the Olympic for Russia.

A Teenager Smiles in Her

Maria Sharapova lists fashion, singing and dancing as her hobbies. She loves reading the novels of Arthur Conan Doyle. Her fondness for sophisticated evening gowns appears at odds with her love of pancakes with chocolate spread and fizzy orange drinks. The dream kept her going and the dream was to be number one.

Exercises

Thinking about the Text

Working in small groups of 4-5 students, go back over the two passages on Santosh Yadav and Maria Sharapova and complete the table given below with relevant phrases or sentences.

Points of Comparison /Contrast	Santosh Yadav	Maria Sharapova
1. Their humble beginning	She was born in the small village of Joniyawas of Rewari District in Haryana, India.	She was born in the frozen plains of Siberia, Russia.
2. Their parent's approach	Her parents disapproved of her going to Delhi for a better education. Eventually, they agreed to fulfill her demands.	Her father worked as much as he could to keep her tennis training going and still took her to the United States.
3. Their will power and strong desire to succeed	Her education was a struggle. She enrolled herself in a mountaineering institute and finally due to her determination scaled Mt. Everest, not once but twice.	She never thought of quitting even in the direst stress. Her will to become number one kept her going.

Points of Comparison /Contrast	Santosh Yadav	Maria Sharapova
4. Evidence of their mental toughness	In addition to her struggle to get a proper education and scaling the Mt. Everest twice, she also saved the life of a fellow climber by sharing her oxygen with her.	She was young and pretty much lonely in the US as her mother could not accompany her. She was ill-treated by other pupils there. This didn't depress her but toughened her mentally.
5. Their patriotism	When she unfurled the tricolour on the roof of the world, her feelings were indescribable. It was a spiritual moment for her. She felt proud as an Indian.	Maria says that though she has spent a long time in the US, she has a Russian Citizenship and her blood is totally Russian. She wanted to represent Russia in the Olympics.

Thinking about Language

I. *Identify the two parts in the sentences below by underlining the part that gives us the information in brackets.*

Q1. Where other girls wore traditional Indian dresses, Santosh preferred shorts. (Contrasts her dress with that of others)

Ans. Where other girls wore traditional Indian dresses, Santosh preferred shorts.

Q2. She left home and got herself enrolled in a school in Delhi. (Tells us what happened after the first action.)

Ans. She left home and got herself enrolled in a school in Delhi.

Q3. She decided to fight the system when the right moment arrived. (Tells us when she was going to fight the system.)

Ans. She decided to fight the system when the right moment arrived.

Q4. Little Maria had not yet celebrated her tenth birthday when she was packed off to train in the United States. (Tells us when Maria was sent to the US)

Ans. Little Maria had not yet celebrated her tenth birthday when she was packed off to train in the United States.

II. *Now rewrite the pairs of sentences given below as one sentence.*

Q 1. Grandfather told me about the old days. All books were printed on paper then.

Ans. Grandfather told me about the old days when all books were printed on paper.

Q 2. What do you do after you finish the book? Perhaps you just throw it away.

Ans. After finishing the book, perhaps you just throw it away.

Q 3. He gave the little girl an apple. He took the computer apart.

Ans. After giving the little girl an apple, he took the computer apart.

Q 4. You have nothing. That makes you very determined.

Ans. Having nothing makes you very determined.

Q 5. I never thought of quitting. I knew what I wanted.

Ans. I never thought of quitting as I knew what I wanted.

Before You Read

A Russian girl, Maria Sharapova, reached the summit of women's tennis when she was barely eighteen. As you read about her, see if you can draw a comparison between her and Santosh Yadav.

Q 1. *Match the following*

something disarming	quickly, almost immediately
at odds with	more calm, confident and in control than people of her age usually are
glamorous attire	in contrast to; not agreeing with
in almost no time	something that makes you feel friendly, taking away your suspiciousness
poised beyond her years	sent off
packed off	attractive and exciting clothes
launched	causing strong feeling of sadness
heart wrenching	started

Ans.

something disarming	something that makes you feel friendly, taking away your suspiciousness
at odds with	in contrast to; not agreeing with
glamorous attire	attractive and exciting clothes
in almost no time	quickly, almost immediately
poised beyond her years	more calm, confident and in control than people of her age usually are
packed off	sent off
launched	started
heart wrenching	causing strong feeling of sadness

***Q* 2.** As you read, look for the answers to these questions

(*i*) Why was Maria sent to the United States?

(*ii*) Why didn't her mother go with her?

(*iii*) What are her hobbies? What does she like?

(*iv*) What moticates her to keep going?

Ans. (*i*) Maria was sent to the United States for her tennis training.

(*ii*) Her mother could not go with her becuase of visa restrictions.

(*iii*) Her hobbies are fashion, singing and dancing. She likes reading the novels of Arthur Conan Doyle. On the other hand, she is fond of sophisticated evening gowns and on the other, of pancakes with chocolate spread and fizzy orange drinks.

(*iv*) Apart from money, the motication to become the number one in the world keeps her going.

9

The Bond of Love

Kenneth Anderson

Chapter Sketch

The chapter talks about love and affection. The narrator brings a baby bear home and gifts him to his wife. As time passed they grow very fond of each other. But the bear was growing big. They give him to the zoo. The narrator's wife and the bear couldn't take the separation and finally the bear is united with her.

Detailed Summary

The Narrator Finds the Bear

The narrator narrates an incident which leads him to the bear. They were passing through the sugarcane fields near Mysore. People were driving away the pigs. They spotted a sloth bear. The narrator didn't want to shoot at it. But his friend did. Then they noticed a baby cub. They ran after it and caught it. The narrator gave him to his wife as a gift.

The Bear Finds New Home

The narrator's wife named him Bruno. She took good care of him. He ate and drank nearly everything. The two pet Alsatian dogs became his buddies. He was free to roam here and there. The family loved him very much.

Bruno Lands Himself in Danger

One day he ate rat poison by mistake. He had to be rushed to the veterinarian. The doctor gave him two injections. Only after that he was able to stand on his feet. Another time he drank some motor oil. But fortunately it had no ill effects.

Bruno Learned Many Things

Bruno grew in size. He equaled the two dogs. He was playful and mischievous. He was very fond of the narrator's wife. She started calling him Baba. He learned a few tricks also. He could wrestle and box and also point a gun using a stick. But as he had grew very big, he had to tied most of the time

Bruno is Sent to the Zoo

The narrator and his son alongwith some friends advise the wife to give Baba to the zoo. She was very reluctant at first but finally though that it was for the best. Hence arrangements were made and Baba was given to the Mysore zoo. The narrator's wife was inconsolable for weeks. It was learned that Baba was also fretting in the zoo. The narrator somehow managed to keep his wife away from the zoo for about three months but she was adamant to meet Baba and hence the narrator gave in.

Baba Comes Back Home

The narrator's wife goes to the zoo. Baba at once recognise her. They sit together for hours. The wife pleads that Baba should be returned to him. After making some arrangements Baba returns home. This time a different kind of set-up is made in the compound for him to stay. Baba was united with his family and thus love and affection prevailed.

Exercises

Thinking about the Text

I. *Given in the box are some headings. Find the relevant paragraphs in the text to match the headings.*

An Orphaned Cub; Bruno's Food-chart; An Accidental Case of Poisoning; Playful Baba; Pain of Separation; Joy of Reunion; A Request to the Zoo; An Island in the Courtyard

Ans. (*i*) An Orphaned Cub – para 3

(*ii*) Bruno's Food-chart – para 6

(*iii*) An Accidental Case of Poisoning – para 8

(*iv*) Playful Baba – para 12

(*v*) Pain of Separation – para 14

(*vi*) Joy of Reunion – para 16

(*vii*) A Request to the Zoo – para 18

(*viii*) An Island in the Courtyard – para 21

II. *Answer the following questions.*

Q 1. "I got him for her by accident."

(*i*) Who says this?

(*ii*) Who do 'him' and 'her' refer to?

(*iii*) What is the incident referred to here?

Ans. (*i*) The narrator says this statement.

(*ii*) Here, 'him' refers to the little sloth bear and 'her' refers to the narrator's wife.

(*iii*) The incident referred to here is the unfortunate killing of the mother bear and catching of the baby-bear.

Q 2. "He stood on his head in delight."

(*i*) Who does 'he' refer to?

(*ii*) Why was he delighted?

Ans. (*i*) Here, 'he' refers to the baby-bear.

(*ii*) He was delighted to see the narrator's wife after a long time.

Q3. "We all missed him greatly; but in a sense we were relieved."

(*i*) Who does 'we all' stand for?

(*ii*) Who did they miss?

(*iii*) Why did they nevertheless feel relieved?

Ans. (*i*) Here, 'we all' stands for the narrator, his wife and his son.

(*ii*) They missed the baby bear Bruno (Baba).

(*iii*) They felt relieved because it was getting very troublesome to keep Bruno at home. That is why they sent him off to a zoo.

III. *Answer the following questions in 30 - 40 words each.*

Q1. On two occasions Bruno ate/drank something that should not be eaten /drunk. What happened to him on these occasions?

Ans. Bruno ate some rat poison on the first occasion. He was nearly paralysed and was critical. They rushed him to the vet and he was finally cured. Later, he drank nearly a gallon of old engine oil. However, it was not that dangerous and no side-effects were observed.

Q2. Was Bruno a loving and playful pet? Why, then, did he have to be sent away?

Ans. Yes, Bruno was a loving and playful pet. With time he had learned a few tricks also. Everybody was attached to him, especially the narrator's wife. He had to be sent away to a zoo because it was becoming difficult to keep him at home.

Q3. How was the problem of what to do with Bruno finally solved?

Ans. On his wife's request, the narrator brought Bruno back from the zoo. At home, they built an island, in the compound, tor the bear. All the stuff that he needed was kept there, even his 'baby' and 'gun'.

Thinking about Language

I. ***Q* 1.** Find these words in the lesson. They all have ie or ei in them.

f__ld	ingred__nts	h__ght	misch__vous
fr__nds	__ghty-seven	rel__ved	p__ce

Ans.

Field	Ingredients	Height	Mischievous
Friends	Eighty-seven	Relieved	Piece

***Q* 2.** Now here are some more words. Complete them with ei or ie. Consult a dictionary if necessary.

bel__ve	rec__ve	w__rd	l__sure	s__ze
w__ght	r__gn	f__gn	gr__f	p__rce

(There is a popular rule of spelling 'i' before 'e' except after 'c'. Check if this rule is true by looking at the words above.)

Ans.

Believe	Receive	Weird	Leisure	Seize
Weight	Reign	Feign	Grief	Pierce

II. *Here are some words with silent letters. Learn their spelling. Your teacher will dictate these words to you. Write them down and underline the silent letters.*

knock	wrestle	walk	wrong
knee	half	honest	daughter
hours	return	hornet	calm
could	sign	island	button

Ans. *The silent words have been underlined as under*

Knock	Wrestle	Walk	Wrong
Knee	Half	Honest	Daughter
Hours	Return	Hornet	Calm
Could	Sign	Island	Button

III. ***Q* 1. The Narrative Present**

Notice the incomplete sentences in the following paragraphs. Here the writer is using incomplete sentences in the narration to make the incident more dramatic or immediate. Can you rewrite the paragraph in complete sentences?

(You can begin The vet and I made a dash back to the car. Bruno was still floundering...)

(*i*) A dash back to car. Bruno still floundering about on his stumps, but clearly weakening rapidly; some vomiting, heavy breathing, with heaving flanks and gaping mouth.

Hold him everybody! In goes the hypodermic? Bruno squeals? 10 cc of the antidote enters his system without a drop being wasted. Then minutes later: condition unchanged! Another 10 cc injected! Ten minutes later: breathing less stertorous ? Bruno can move his arms and legs a little although he can not stand yet. Thirty minutes later: Bruno gets up and has a great feed! He looks at us disdainfully, as much as to say, 'What's barium carbonate to a big black bear like me?' Bruno is still eating.

Ans. The vet and I made a dash back to the car. Bruno was still floundering about on his stumps. He was clearly weakening. This was evident from some vomiting, heavy breathing, with heaving flanks and his gaping mouth. The vet told us to hold him. Then he pushed in the hypodermic in Bruno's arm. He squealed but the antidote entered his system without a drop being wasted.

After three minutes his condition was still unchanged. The vet pushed in another 10 c.c. Ten minutes later his breathing got a bit normal and he could move his arms and legs. Then after thirty minutes, Bruno was fine and had food. He had a disdainful look in his eyes, as if he was asking, "What's barium carbonate to a big black bear like me?" He kept eating.

***Q* 2. Adverbs**

Find the adverbs in the passage below. (You've read about adverbs in Unit 1.)

We thought that everything was over when suddenly a black sloth bear came out panting in the hot sun. Now I will not shoot a sloth bear wantonly but, unfortunately for the poor beast, one of my companions did not feel that way about it, and promptly shot the bear on the spot.

Ans. Suddenly, Wantonly, Unfortunately, Promptly

(*i*) Complete the following sentences, using a suitable adverb ending in _ly.

(a) Rana does her homework ______________.

(b) It rains __________ in Mumbai in June.

(c) He does his work ____________.

(d) The dog serves his master ____________.

Ans. (*i*) (a) Rana does her homework timely.

(b) It rains heavily in Mumbai in June.

(c) He does his work properly.

(d) The dog serves his master faithfully.

(*ii*) Choose the most suitable adverbs or adverbial phrases and complete the following sentences.

(a) We should ___________get down from a moving train. (never, sometimes, often)

(b) I was __________ in need of support after my poor performance. (badly, occasionally, sometimes).

(c) Rita met with an accident. The doctor examined her ____________. (suddenly, seriously, immediately)

Ans. (*ii*) (a) We should never get down from a moving train.

(b) I was badly in need of support after my poor performance.

(c) Rita met with an accident. The doctor examined her immediately.

***Q* 3.** Take down the following scrambled version of a story, that your teacher will dictate to you, with appropriate punctuation marks. Then, read the scrambled story carefully and try to rewrite it rearranging the incidents.

A grasshopper, who was very hungry, saw her and said, "When did you get the corn? I am dying of hunger." She wanted to dry them. It was a cold winter's day and an ant was bringing out some grains of corn from her home. She had gathered the corn in summer.

"I was singing all day," answered the grasshopper.

"If you sang all summer," said the ant, "you can dance all winter."

"What were you doing?" asked the ant again.

The grasshopper replied, "I was too busy."

"I collected it in summer," said the ant.

"What were you doing in summer? Why did you not store some corn?"

Ans. It was a cold winter's day and an ant was bringing out some grains of corn from her home. She had gathered the corn in summer. She wanted to dry them. A grasshopper, who was very hungry, saw her and said, "When did you get the corn? I am dying of hunger."

"I collected it in summer," said the ant. "What were you doing in summer? Why did you not store some corn?" The grasshopper replied, "I was too busy." "What were you doing?" asked the ant again. "I was singing all day," answered the grasshopper. "If you sang all summer," said the ant, "you can dance all winter."

10

Kathmandu

Vikram Seth

Chapter Sketch

The lesson takes us to the beautiful place that is Kathmandu. It is basically a description of its two most famous temples. One is of the Hindus- The Pashupatinath temple. The other is a Buddhist shrine- The Baudhnath stupa.

Detailed Summary

Entrance for Hindus Only

A sign at the Pashupatinath temple proclaims that entrance is allowed only to the Hindus. Utter chaos prevails as throngs and throngs of people along with all sorts of animals roam around the area. Everybody seems to be making way to the main temple. The narrator notices some Western devotees trying to enter the temple and having a quarrel with the guards. They are not allowed as they are not Hindus. Monkeys can also be seen fighting.

The End of Kaliyug

The Bagmati River flows besides the temple. There is a small shrine half submersed on the river bank. The people believe that one day when the shrine wholly comes out of the water, then the goddess inside it will escape and thus bring an end to the evil period of Kaliyug.

The Baudhnath Stupa

Unlike the Pashupatinath temple, there is stillness at the Baudhnath stupa. It has a immense white dome ringed with roads. There are shops of Tibetan immigrants and the place has no crowds.

Narrator Describes Kathmandu

Kathmandu seems to be a busy place. Streets are crowded with fruit sellers, flute sellers, etc. Shops have all kinds of Western stuff. All types of commodities are sold here. The narrator is busy in his own musings. He is enjoying himself. But is also planning to go back as he is homesick. So, instead of the train he is determined to take a flight back.

The Music of Flute

The narrator then notices a flute seller in the market. It appears that he is in love with the music of flute. He describes the seen quite vividly. It is music to his ears. He then explains that no culture has remained untouched of the reed pipe or the recorder as he calls it. He was actually surprised at the thought that he found it this much intriguing.

Exercises

Thinking about the Text

I. *Answer these questions in one or two words or in short phrases.*

Q 1. Name the two temples the author visited in Kathmandu.

Ans. The two temples that the author visited in Kathmandu were the Pashupatinath temple and the Baudhnath stupa.

Q 2. The writer says, "All this I wash down with Coca Cola." What does 'all this' refer to?

Ans. 'All this refers to a bar of marzipan, a corn-on-the-cob roasted in a charcoal stove (rubbed with salt, chilli powder and lemon), a couple of love story comics and a Reader's Digest.

***Q* 3.** What does Vikram Seth compare to the quills of a porcupine?

Ans. Vikram Seth compares the fifty or sixty bansuris protruding in all directions from to the quills of a porcupine.

***Q* 4.** Name five kinds of flutes.

Ans. The reed *neh*, the recorder the Japanese *shakuhachi*, the deep *bansuri* of Hindustani classical music, the clear or breathy flutes of South America and the high-pitched Chinese flutes.

II. *Answer each question in a short paragraph.*

***Q* 1.** What difference does the author note between the flute seller and the other hawkers?

Ans. The author noticed the difference in the way the two were selling their respective products. The fruit seller blared out his wares while the flute seller sold the flutes in a slow, meditative and without excessive show.

***Q* 2.** What is the belief at Pashupatinath about the end of Kaliyug?

Ans. At Pashupatinath, there is a small shrine on the bank of Bagmati river that is half immersed in water. The belief is that when it emerges fully, the goddess inside will escape and the evil period of Kaliyug will end on the earth.

***Q* 3.** The author has drawn powerful images and pictures. Pick out three examples each of

(*i*) the atmosphere of 'febrile confusion' outside the temple of Pashupatinath (for example some people trying to get the priest's attention are elbowed aside...)

(*ii*) the things he sees

(iii) the sounds he hears

Ans. (*i*) Many worshippers trying to get the priest's attention were elbowed aside by others pushing their way to the front. On the main gate, a party of saffron-clad Westerners struggled for permission to enter as only Hindus were allowed to enter the temple. A fight broke out between two monkeys. One was chasing the other, who jumped onto a shivalinga, then ran screaming around the temples and down to the river,the holy Bagmati.

(*ii*) He saw that the Baudhnath stupa had an immense white dome, which was ringed by a road. Small shops were there on the outeredge where felt bags, Tibetan prints and silver jewellery could be bought. There were no crowds there. On the busiest streets of Kathmandu, he saw fruit sellers, flute sellers, hawkers of postcards, shops selling Western cosmetics, film rolls, chocolate, copper utensils and Nepalese antiques.

(*iii*) The sounds he heard were film songs that were blaring out from the radios, car horns, bicycle bells, vendors shouting out their wares. He also listened to flute music, calling it the most universal and most particular of sounds.

III. *Answer the following questions in not more than 100-150 words each.*

Q 1. Compare and contrast the atmosphere in and around the Baudhnath shrine with the Pashupatinath temple.

Ans. The atmosphere at Pashupatinath temple was one of noise, chaos and confusion. Worshippers were trying to get the priest's attention; others were pushing their way to the front; saffron-clad. Westerners were trying to enter the temple; monkeys were fighting and adding to the general noise; a corpse was being cremated on the banks of the river Bagmati; washerwomen were at their work, while their children were bathing. In contrast, the Baudhnath stupa was "a haven of quietness in the busy streets around". There was a sense of stillness and serenity about the Buddhist shrine.

Q 2. How does the author describe Kathmandu's busiest streets?

Ans. Along Kathmandu's narrowest and busiest streets, there were small shrines and flower-adorned deities. Apart from these, there were fruit sellers, flute sellers, hawkers of postcards, shops selling Western cosmetics, film rolls, chocolate, copper utensils and Nepalese antiques. The author heard film songs that were blaring out from the radios, sounds of car horns and bicycle bells, vendors shouting out their wares. He also saw a flute seller with many bansuris. He contrasts the serene music produced by the flute seller with the cries of the hawkers.

Q3. "To hear any flute is to be drawn into the commonality of all mankind." Why does the author say this?

Ans. The author considers flute music to be "the most universal and most particular" of all music. There is no culture that does not have its flute. Each kind of flute has a specific fingering and compass and "weaves its own associations". Still, for the author, to hear any flute is "to be drawn into the commonality of all mankind". In spite of their differences, every flute produces music with the help of the human breath. Similarly, in spite of the differences in caste, culture, religion, region, all human beings are the same, with the same living breath running through all of them.

Thinking about Language

I. *Read the following sentences carefully to understand the meaning of the italicised phrases. Then match the phrasal verbs in Column A with their meanings in Column B.*

1. A communal war *broke out* when the princess was abducted by the neighbouring prince.
2. The cockpit *broke off* from the plane during the plane crash.
3. The car *broke down* on the way and we were left stranded in the jungle.
4. The dacoit *broke away* from the police as they took him to court.
5. The brothers *broke up* after the death of the father.
6. The thief *broke into* our house when we were away.

	A		B
(i)	break out	(a)	to come apart due to force
(ii)	break off	(b)	end a relationship
(iii)	break down	(c)	break and enter illegally; unlawful trespassing
(iv)	break away (from someone)	(d)	of start suddenly, (usually a fight, a war or a disease)
(v)	break up	(e)	to escape form someone's grip
(vi)	break into	(f)	stop working

Ans.

	A		B
(i)	break out	(d)	of start suddenly, (usually a fight, a war or a disease)
(ii)	break off	(a)	to come apart due to force
(iii)	break down	(f)	stop working
(iv)	break away (from someone)	(e)	to escape form someone's grip
(v)	break up	(b)	end a relationship
(vi)	break into	(c)	break and enter illegally; unlawful trespassing

II. ***Q* 1.** Use the suffixes _ion or _tion to form nouns from the following verbs. Make the necessary changes in the spellings of the words.

Example proclaim – proclamation

cremate ______	act ______	exhaust ______
invent ______	tempt ____	immigrate _____
direct ______	meditate _____	imagine _______
dislocate _____	associate ____	dedicate _______

Ans. cremate : cremation act : action exhaust : exhaustion

invent : invention tempt : temptation immigrate : immigration

direct : direction meditate : meditation imagine : imagination

dislocate : dislocation associate : association

dedicate : dedication

***Q* 2.** Now fill in the blanks with suitable words from the ones that you have formed.

(*i*) Mass literacy was possible only after the ________ of the printing machine.

(*ii*) Ramesh is unable to tackle the situation as he lacks ________.

(*iii*) I could not resist the _________ to open the letter.

(*iv*) Hardwork and _________ are the main keys to success.

(*v*) The children were almost fainting with _________ after being made to stand in the sun.

Ans. (*i*) Mass literacy was possible only after the invention of the printing machine.

(*ii*) Ramesh is unable to tackle the situation as he lacks imagination.

(*iii*) I could not resist the temptation to open the letter.

(*iv*) Hardwork and dedication are the main keys to success.

(*v*) The children were almost fainting with exhaustion after being made to stand in the sun.

III. *Punctuation*

Use capital letter, full stops, question marks, commas and inverted commas wherever necessary in the following paragraph.

an arrogant lion was wandering though the jungle one day he asked the tiger who is stronger than you you O lion replied the tiger who is more fierce than a leopard asked the lion you sir replied the leopard he marched upto an elephant and asked the same question the elephant picked him up in his trunk swung him in the air and threw him down look said the lion there is no need to get mad just because you don't know the answer.

Ans. An arrogant lion was wandering through the jungle one day. He asked the tiger, "Who is stronger than you?" "You, O lion!" replied the tiger. "Who is more fierce than a leopard?" asked the lion. "You sir," replied the leopard. He marched up to an elephant and asked the same question. The elephant picked him up in his trunk, swung him in the air and threw him down. "Look," said the lion, "there is no need to get mad just because you don't know the answer".

IV. ***Q* 1.** Fill in the blanks with the correct form of the verb in brackets.

(*i*) The heart is a pump that _____(send) the blood circulating through our body. The pumping action _____(take place) when the left ventricle of the heart ______ (contract). This ______ (force) the blood out into the arteries, which _____ (expand) to receive the oncoming blood.

(*ii*) The African lungfish can live without water for up to four years. During drought, it _____(dig) a pit and ______(enclose) itself in a capsule of slime and earth, leaving a tiny opening for air. The capsule ______ (dry) and ____________(harden), but when rain _______(come), the mud ______ (dissolve) and the lungfish ______(swim) away.

(*iii*) **Mahesh** We have to organise a class party for our teacher. _______(Do) anyone play an instrument?

Vipul Rohit _____(play) the flute.

Mahesh ______(Do) he also act?

Vipul No, he ______(compose) music.

Mahesh That's wonderful!

Ans. (*i*) The heart is a pump that sends the blood circulating through our body. The pumping action takes place when the left ventricle of the heart contracts. This forces the blood out into the arteries, which expands to receive the on coming blood.

(*ii*) The African lungfish can live without water for up to four years. During drought, it digs a pit and encloses itself in a capsule of slime and Earth, leaving a tiny opening for air. The capsule dries and hardens, but when rain comes, the mud dissolves and the lungfish swims away.

(*iii*) **Mahesh** We have to organise a class party for our teacher. Does anyone play an instrument?

Vipul Rohit plays the flute.

Mahesh Does he also act?

Vipul No, he doesn't composes music.

Mahesh That's wonderful!

11

If I Were You

Douglas James

Chapter Sketch

An intruder enters the house of Gerrard. He wants to kill him and take his identity. He had killed a cop and was tired of running. He wanted a new identity. But Gerrard is no regular person. He is a playwright with a mind of a genius. The intruder didn't know this. He had heard that he was a mystery man. Gerrard uses his wits and saves his life.

Detailed Summary

Intruder in Gerrard's House

The intruder entered Gerrard's house. Gerrard was about to leave for his rehearsal. The intruder told him that he was there to kill him. He had killed a cop and was tired of running. So, he wanted a new identity. He chose Gerrard to be the appropriate victim for this.

Gerrard Keeps His Cool

Gerrard is bit surprised but tries to keep his cool. He gets the intruder talking and thus delay his decision to kill Gerrard. The intruder starts asking him questions to which Gerrard replies quite cunningly so that he can use more time of his. The intruder keeps on threatening him that he will surely shoot.

The Intruder had not done his Homework

The intruder pretended that he had some information about Gerrard. Gerrard seemed to realise that he doesn't know much about his work and his whereabouts. He started manipulating the talks.

Gerrard Tries to Talk his Way Out

Gerrard tries to talk his way out by saying that the intruder can never imitate him for whole life. He needs to learn a lot about him. But the foolish intruder imitates his voice and gives a description of how he would dress himself and behave. So, that people may think that he is Gerrard.

Gerrard Fools the Intruder

Gerrard then plays a trick. He asks the intruder that why does he think that Gerrard is a mystery man. He tells him that he is a criminal himself and he is about to escape. The bag contains make up material to disguise himself. The intruder falls for the trick when the telephone rings. Gerrard rushes him and locks him up. Thus, Gerrard's wits save his life.

Thinking about the Text

I. *Answer these questions*

Q 1. "At last a sympathetic audience."

(*i*) Who says this?

(*ii*) Why does he say it?

(*iii*) Is he sarcastic or serious?

Ans. (*i*) Gerrard says this.

(*ii*) He says it because the intruder had asked him to talk about himself.

(*iii*) He was being sarcastic. The audience, *i.e.*, the intruder was in no ways sympathetic. In fact, he told Gerrard, at gunpoint, to talk about himself so that he could use the information to further his own interests.

Q 2. **Why does the intruder choose Gerrard as the man whose identity he wants to take on?**

Ans. The intruder chooses Gerrard as the man whose identity he wanted to take on because he was of the same build as Gerrard. Also, as Vincent Charles Gerrard, he would be free to go places and do nothing. He could eat well and sleep without having to be ready to run away at the sight of a cop.

Q 3. **"I said it with bullets".**

(*i*) Who says this?

(*ii*) What does it mean?

(*iii*) Is it the truth? What is the speaker's reason for saying this?

Ans. (*i*) Gerrard says this.

(*ii*) It means that when things went wrong with him, he had committed a murder and got away. Here, "I said it with bullets" means that he fired at someone to escape.

(*iii*) No, it was not the truth. Gerrard said so because he wanted the intruder to believe that he too was dangerous. The intruder would have killed him if he had not lied about his identity. He told him that he himself was a crook; that he had also killed someone and escaped. However, his partner had been caught and he had not burnt the papers that should have been burnt.

Therefore, the cops were after him too and this meant that the intruder would still not be safe even after taking on Gerrard's identity.

Q 4. **What is Gerrard's profession? Quote the parts of the play that support your answer.**

Ans. Gerrard could have been a theatrical artist, perhaps a playwright. There are several parts in the play which suggest that he had something to do with theatre. When he saw the intruder, he said "This is all very melodramatic, not very original, perhaps, but..." When the intruder asked him to talk about himself, he said "At last a sympathetic audience!".

He also asked the intruder "Are you American or is that merely a clever imitation?" Then, when the intruder had told him his plan of killing him and taking over his identity, he said "In most melodramas the villain is foolish enough to delay his killing long enough to be frustrated." Later, he again said "I said, you were luckier than most melodramatic villains." When he told the intruder about his false identity in order to save himself, he told him "That's a disguise outfit; false moustaches and what not". Finally, after locking him up, he picked up the phone and said "Sorry, I can't let you have the props in time for rehearsal, I've had a spot of bother—quite amusing. I think I'll put it in my next play."

Q 5. "You'll soon stop being smart".

(*i*) Who says this?

(*ii*) Why does the speaker say it?

(*iii*) What according to the speaker will stop Gerrard from being smart?

Ans. (*i*) The intruder says this.

(*ii*) When Gerrard did not show any signs of being perturbed by the intruder's presence, the intruder responded by saying "Trying to be calm and — er —". He stopped and fumbled for words and then, Gerrard completed his sentence by saying "Nonchalant is your word, I think". Peeved at the smartness displayed by Gerrard, the intruder said that Gerrard would stop being smartonce he knew what was going to happen to him.

(*iii*) According to the intruder, Gerrard would stop being smartonce he knew what was going to happen to him. The intruder's plan was to kill Gerrard and take over his identity. He felt that when Gerrard would know this, he would stop being smart and start getting scared.

Q 6. "They can't hang me twice".

(*i*) Who says this?

(*ii*) Why does the speaker say it?

Ans. (*i*) The intruder says this.

(*ii*) The intruder had been telling Gerrard that he had murdered one man and that he would not shy away from murdering him too. This is because the police could not hang him twice for two murders.

Q 7. "A mystery I propose to explain." What is the mystery the speaker proposes to explain?

Ans. The mystery that Gerrard proposed to explain was the story he made up to dodge the intruder and escape him. The story was that Gerrard himself was a criminal like the intruder. He asked why else would he not meet any trades people and was all over different places. When things went wrong with him, he had committed a murder and got away. Unfortunately, one of his men had been arrested and certain things were found which his men should have burnt. He said that he was expecting some trouble that night and therefore, his bag was packed and he was ready to escape.

Q 8. "This is your big surprise."

(*i*) Where has this been said in the play?

(*ii*) What is the surprise?

Ans. (*i*) The given line was spoken twice in the play. First, it was spoken by the intruder when he revealed to Gerrard why he was there and what he was going to do with him. On the second occasion, it was spoken by Gerrard when he was about to reveal his made up story to the intruder.

(*ii*) When the intruder said this line, the surprise was that he was going to kill Gerrard and take over his identity. He told him that as Vincent Charles Gerrard, he would be free to go places and do nothing. He could eat well and sleep without having to be ready to run away at the sight of a cop.When Gerrard said this line, the surprise was his made-up story about himself.

The story was that Gerrard himself was a criminal like the intruder. When things went wrong with him, he had committed a murder and got away. Unfortunately, one of his men was arrested and certain things were found, which his men should have burnt. He said that he was expecting some trouble that night and therefore, his bag was packed and he was ready to escape.

Thinking about Language

I. *Consult your dictionary and choose the correct word from the pairs given in brackets.*

Q 1. The (site, cite) of the accident was (ghastly/ghostly).

Ans. The site of the accident was ghastly.

Q 2. Our college (principle/principal) is very strict.

Ans. Our college principal is very strict.

Q 3. I studied (continuously/continually) for eight hours.

Ans. I studied continuously for eight hours.

Q 4. The fog had an adverse (affect/effect) on the traffic.

Ans. The fog had an adverse effect on the traffic.

Q 5. Cezanne, the famous French painter, was a brilliant (artist/artiste).

Ans. Cezanne, the famous French painter, was a brilliant artist.

Q 6. The book that you gave me yesterday is an extraordinary (collage/college) of science fiction and mystery.

Ans. The book that you gave me yesterday is an extraordinary collage of science fiction and mystery.

Q 7. Our school will (host/hoist) an exhibition on cruelty to animals and wildlife conservation.

Ans. Our school will host an exhibition on cruelty to animals and wildlife conservation.

Q 8. Screw the lid tightly onto the top of the bottle and (shake/shape) well before using the contents.

Ans. Screw the lid tightly onto the top of the bottle and shake well before using the contents.

II. *Irony is when we say one thing but mean another, usually the opposite of what we say. When someone makes a mistake and you say, "Oh! That was clever!" that is irony. You're saying 'clever' to mean 'not clever'.*

Expressions we often use in an ironic fashion are

- Oh, wasn't that clever!/Oh that was clever!
- You have been a great help, I must say!
- You've got yourself into a lovely mess, haven't you?
- Oh, very funny!/How funny!

We use a slightly different tone of voice when we use these words ironically.

Read the play carefully and find the words and expressions Gerrard uses in an ironic way. Then say what these expressions really mean. Two examples have been given below. Write down three such expressions along with what they really mean.

What the author says	What he means
Why, this is a surprise. Mr—er—	He pretends that the intruder is a social visitor whom he is welcoming. In this way he hides his fear.
At last a sympathetic audience!	Her pretends that the intruder wants to listen to him, whereas actually the intruder wants to find out information for his own use.

Ans.

What the author says	What he means
You won't kill me for a very good reason.	Gerrard was just pretending to have a 'very good reason'. However, there was no such reason.
In most melodramas the villain is foolish enough to delay his killing long enough to be frustrated. You are much luckier.	Gerrard said that the 'villain' takes to long a time to make the killing and ends up being at the wrong end. However, the intruder had been quite smart and lucky for not killing Gerrard and high-jacking his identity. As we know, Gerrard then tells him a cooked up story and the intruder turns out to be like the foolish villain of most melodramas.
Sorry I can't let you have props in time for rehearsal, I've had a spot of bother—quite amusing.	The 'spot of bother' that Gerrard found 'quite amusing' was actually a life-threatening situation. He was being held at gunpoint by a murderer who wanted to take his identity.

Poetry

6

No Men Are Foreign

James Kirkup

Chapter Sketch

Through the poem 'No Men Are Foreign' the poet 'James Kirkup' gives a very nice message of humanity. We have seen many people in our lives who don't look like us, belong to different country and speak a different language. They may even seem strange to us. But apart from the exterior, we are all the same for we are all human.

Detailed Summary

No Men are Strange

The poet wants us to remember fact that no men are strange and no country is foreign because even if the people, living on this world divided by borders, dress differently, we have the same body. The land on which our 'other' brothers walk is same as the earth on which we all lie.

Not Different from Our Own

'They' also know the importance of sun, air and water. 'They' too need them to grow their food. We all equally love peace and hate war. Here war has been compared to winter because like war causes destruction similarly in winter it becomes hard for the harvesting and scarcity occurs. 'They' do labour like we do. Their day-to-day work and routine is not different from ours.

Eyes Like Ours

'They' have eyes like ours that wake or sleep. It probably means that the so called others dream the way we do. 'They' also have the same desires and dreams. The poet also conveys the message that all strength can be won by love. Everywhere we go, we will find common life. Life as same as ours that all can recognise and understand.

Hate will Harm Us

The poet wants us to remember that whenever we are told to hate our brothers or we fight with them and raise arms against them, it is ourselves that we shall dispossess, betray and condemn. Hence, through this passage the poet wants us to spread love and not hatred.

'We' have the Power

When we wage wars against each other, we pollute the air which is our own, we harm our brothers and we defile the earth which is our own everywhere. We are humans, we have the power and we must put it to the right use. Remember, none is foreign or strange.

Exercises

Thinking about the Poem

Q1. (*i*) "Beneath all uniforms..." What uniforms do you think the poet is speaking about ?

(*ii*) How does the poet suggest that all people on earth are the same ?

Ans. (*i*) The poet is probably speaking about the different kinds of attire that people wear. Every country has its own 'uniforms' which are unique to them. They make us look different.

(*ii*) The poet says that even though people of different nationalitics look different from the outside, but we all are human beings. We have the same body whose needs are also the same.

Q2. In stanza 1, find five ways in which we all are alike. Pick out the words.

Ans. *Following ways we all are alike in stanza 1*

(*i*) No men are strange.

(*ii*) No countries are foreign.

(*iii*) A single body breathes beneath all uniforms.
(*iv*) The land is the same everywhere.
(*v*) The land is the same where all shall lie.

The words are—A single body breathes the earth is like this etc.

Q3. How many common features can you find in stanza 2? Pick out the words.

Ans. *Following common features can be found in stanza 2*

(*i*) They are aware of sun, air and water
(*ii*) They are fed by peaceful harvests.
(*iii*) Their hands are ours.
(*iv*) The lines of hands.
(*v*) A labour not different from our own.

The words are—They, too, are, aware of sun, air and water; are fed by peaceful harvests, their hands are ours etc.

Q4. "... whenever we are told to hate our brothers..." When do you think this happens ? Why ? Who 'tells' us ? Should we do as we are told at such times ? What does the poet say ?

Ans. The perperators of wars, who have selfish motives to conquer and subjugate others incite 'brothers' to hate each other. They are the ones who tell us to prepare wars.

No, we should not do things their way. Other countrymen are like us only. As the poet says that, no men are foreign and no countries strange.

The Duck and the Kangaroo

Edward Lear

Chapter Sketch

While this poem seems to be non-sensical, there seems to be another lesson to be learned. The duck is discontent with life and sees the kangaroo's life as being more exciting and adventurous. After some negotiations both agree to certain terms and the kangaroo agrees to give a ride to the duck. But how long can such an arrangement survive.

Detailed Summary

The Discontent Duck

The duck is fascinated by the kangaroo's long jumps. Actually the long hops of the kangaroo are nothing but a representation of a distinct and adventurous lifestyle. The duck then ridicules its mediocre existence in the 'nasty pond'. It wishes to see the worlds beyond like the kangaroo.

The Duck's Wish

The duck displayed a desire to ride on the back of the kangaroo. It said that it would sit on the back of the kangaroo and will not utter anything. It reiterates its desire to see the places that the kangaroo roamed into.

The Kangaroo's Objection

The kangaroo considered the duck's appeal and said that he had a little objection. The kangaroo's objection is that the duck's webbed feet are cold and damp and it would give him rheumatic fever.

The Duck's Arrangements

The duck assures the kangaroo that several pairs of warm socks, a cloak and a cigar should keep the cold at bay. This seems silly as the duck is taking on features not natural to its nature. In a sense the duck has to make changes not true to self in order to experience the life of another.

Who is Happy?

Now, the kangaroo is convinced and ready to let the duck take a piggy-back ride. It allows the duck to sit still on its tail. Finally their joyride begins and they encircle the Earth three times! However, the poet at the end gives some fodder for one's mind by asking that who benefitted most from such an arrangement.

8

On Killing a Tree

Gieve Patel

Chapter Sketch

In the poem 'On Killing a Tree', the poet talks about the fact that it is not easy to kill a tree. It has taken years to grow. Its roots are deep. A simple jab of knife wouldn't be enough. It will continue to grow until its root are exposed to the sunlight and air.

Detailed Summary

How the Tree has Grown?

In the opening stanza, the poet emphasises the fact that it takes much time to kill a tree and a simple jab of the knife would not be enough.

The tree has grown slowly consuming the earth. It fed upon its crust. For years it kept absorbing sunlight, air and water. Only after this it became a tree.

The Tree will Expand Again

In the second stanza, the poet says that even the pain given by hacking and chopping wont kill a tree. The bleeding bark will heal and small green branches will rise close to the ground. The twigs will expand again to former size if kept unchecked.

The Root of the Tree

In the third stanza, the poet tells the reason of the tree's strength. To kill a tree one needs to pull out its root, out of the anchoring earth. It is to be roped, tied and snapped out or pulled out entirely. The most sensitive part of the tree yet the reason of its strength needs to be exposed. It was hidden for years inside the earth.

Then it is Done

The tree will choke as it would not be able to feed itself. The scorching sun and air will play their part. The green leaves will fall. It will get brown and hard. Then, it will get twisted and dried up. Finally, the tree will die.

Exercises

Thinking about the Poem

Q1. Can a "simple jab of the knife" kill a tree? Why not?

Ans. No, a simple jab of the knife wouldn't be enough to kill a tree because it will heal itself.

Q2. How has the tree grown to its full size? List the words suggestive of its life and activity.

Ans. The tree has grown to its full size slowly consuming the earth and rising out of it. If fed upon the earth's crust for years, absorbing sunlight, air and water. The words are consuming, rising, feeding and absorbing.

Q3. What is the meaning of "bleeding bark"? What makes it bleed?

Ans. The "bleeding bark" refers to the bark of the tree which gives out a liquid after it is cut or hurt. Hacking and chopping the tree make its bark bleed.

Q4. The poet says "No" in the beginning of the third stanza. What does he mean by this?

Ans. The poet says "No" in the beginning of the third stanza to highlight the fact that a tree cannot be killed by merely with a jab of a knife or hacking and chopping.

Q5. What is the meaning of "anchoring earth" and "earth cave"?

Ans. "Anchoring earth" refers to the soil in which the roots of the tree are kept hidden. "Earth cave" also refers to the same. The soil and the roots of the tree form a very tight grip, like an anchor it keeps it rooted. Like a cave gives shelter, similarly, the earth gives shelter to the roots.

Q6. What does he mean by "the strength of the tree exposed"?

Ans. The strength of the tree are its roots. They keep it anchored to the earth. They are the provider of nutrients for the tree. When the tree is pulled out of the earth's soil, these are exposed.

Q7. What finally kills the tree?

Ans. The tree is killed when its roots are exposed to the outside. The scorching heat of the sun and air choke it. It loses all it leaves and gets brown. Twisting, hardening and drying, it dies.

9

The Snake Trying

W.W.E. Ross

Chapter Sketch

Whenever we hear the word snake, an image of a poisonous and fearsome beast flashes through our mind. They are symbols of death. But the poet sees that this is not the case always. In this poem the snake is itself a victim and tries to escape.

Detailed Summary

The Snake Trying to Escape

The snake is trying to escape as someone is chasing him with a stick. He makes swift, steep turns. The poet finds beauty in his sudden curved movements.

The Poet Appeals to Let Him Go

The snakes appears to glide on water. He is trying to be safe from the stroke of the stick. The poet appeals that he should be allowed to go and hide in the plants as he is harmless. The small green snake appears to be non-poisonous and hence it cannot hurt even children.

The Snake Vanishes

The snake was lying in sand unmoved until it was observed and the observer ran after it with a stick. The snake was quick and finally vanishes in the ripples among the green slim reeds.

Exercises

Thinking about the Poem

***Q*1.** What is the snake trying to escape from?

Ans. The snake tries to escape from someone who is chasing him with a stick. The snake is under threat and is trying to save his life.

***Q*2.** Is it a harmful snake ? What is its colour?

Ans. No, the snake is not harmful. It is green in colour.

***Q*3.** The poet finds the snake beautiful. Find the words he uses to convey its beauty .

Ans. The words that convey snake's beauty are 'beautiful and graceful, glides, 'thin long body', small and green'.

***Q*4.** What does the poet wish for the snake ?

Ans. The poet wishes that the snake must be allowed to go unhurt because it is harmless even to children.

***Q*5.** Where was the snake before anyone saw it and chased it away? Where does the snake disappear?

Ans. The snake was lying along the sand when someone noticed it and chased it away. The snake tried to save his life and vanished in the ripples among the green slim reeds.

10

A Slumber Did My Spirit Seal

William Wordsworth

Chapter Sketch

Ths short poem written by 'William Wordsworth' is about the death of a loved one. The loss has made the poet sad. But he realises that death is inevitable and in a sense is quite peaceful for his loved one. Now, the passing of time cannot affect her.

Detailed Summary

The Poet's Loss

The poet says that a deep sleep has sealed his spirits. He has no fears now. His loved one who has died seems like a thing that cannot feel anything. The passing of years cannot affect her now.

The Poet is in Peace

The dead loved one has no motion or force. She can neither hear nor see. The poet appears to be in peace as his loved one will no longer be affected by the worldly things. Earth's movement will not affect her as she has now become a part of it.

Exercises

Thinking about the Poem

Q1. "A slumber did my spirit seal", says the poet. That is, a deep sleep 'closed off' his soul (or mind). How does the poet react to his loved one's death? Does he feel bitter grief? Or does he feel a great peace?

Ans. The poet is very grieved at the loss of his loved one. He appears to be totally shocked by the sad state of his life. Then, he realises that his loved one is at peace now. Nothing can affect her. This makes him feel contended.

Q2. The passing of time will no longer affect her, says the poet. Which lines of the poem say this?

Ans. The lines that suggest that the passing of time will no longer affect the poet's beloved are "She seemed a thing that could not feel—The touch of earthly years".

Q3. How does the poet imagine her to be, after death? Does he think of her as a person living in a very happy state (a 'heaven')? Or does he see her now as a part of nature? In which lines of the poem do you find your answer?

Ans. The poet imagines her to be indifferent to the earthly affairs. He thinks that she is happy, but has become a part of nature. "Rolled round in earth's diurnal course/With rocks and stones and trees," has this answer.

6

Weathering the Storm in Ersama

Harsh Mander

Chapter Sketch

The story is a poignant account of the ordeals faced by the protagonist, Prashant and many families whose lives were completely devastated by the storm that hit Orissa on October 27, 1999.

Detailed Summary

The Storm Hits Ersama

On October 27, 1999, seven years after his mother's death, Prashant had gone to the block headquarters of Ersama, a small town in Coastal Orissa to spend the day with a friend. In the evening, a dark and menacing storm quickly gathered. Prashant had never seen such fury of the winds. The 350 km per hour wind uprooted the ancient trees and the storm washed away the people and the houses.

Havoc All Around

For the next thirty six hours the water kept rising. To escape the waters rising in the house, Prashant and his friend's family had taken refuge on the roof. Prashant could never forget the devastation that he witnessed that day. A raging, deadly, brown sheet of water covered everything as far as the eye could see; only fractured cement houses still stood in a few places. Bloated animal carcasses and human corpses floated in every direction.

Prashant Tries to Reach his Family

They were stranded on the roof for the next two days. Prashant was concerned about his family. After the water receded, Prashant set out to seek his family even when the situation was still dangerous. He equipped himself with a long, sturdy stick and then started on his 18 km expedition back to his village through the swollen flood waters. After some distance, he was relieved to find two friends of his uncle who were also returning to their village. They decided to move ahead together. The scenes on the way were very horrific. Animal and human carcasses came floating in their way.

Prashant Reunites with his Family

Finally, Prashant reached his village, Kalikuda. The cyclone had destroyed his home. Prashant decided to go to the Red Cross shelter to look for his family. Prashant was relieved to find all his family members.

Prashant—A New Leader

The whole village was destroyed. Many people had died. Prashant had sensed the deathly grief around him and decided to step up as the new leader of the village in a time of despondence. Prashant, alongwith some elderly, pressurised the merchant to part away with his rice. Then after gathering the firewood, food was prepared and the whole village ate a meal after four days. He then organised a team of youth volunteers to clean the shelter of filth, urine, vomit and floating carcasses and to tend to the wounds and fractures of the many who had been injured.

Relief was on the Way

On the fifth day, a military helicopter flew over the shelter and dropped some food parcels. It then did not return. The youth task force gathered empty utensils from the shelter.

Then they deputed the children to lie in the sand left by the waters around the shelter with these utensils on their stomachs to communicate to the passing helicopters that they were hungry. The message got through and after that the helicopter made regular rounds of the shelter, airdropping food and other basic needs.

Prashant—An Unlikely Messiah

He noticed that many of the children were orphaned. He organised woman groups to look after them. But the people were sinking deeper and deeper into grief. Prashant was quick to realise this and he persuaded the women to start working in the food-for-work programme started by an Non-Government Organisation (NGO) and for the children he organised sporting events. The community decided that the widow and orphan institutions were of no use. Instead, they believed that orphans should be resettled in their own community itself, possibly in new foster families made up of childless widows and children without adult care.
Prashant was the hero under the direst stress.

Exercises

Q1. What havoc has the super cyclone wreaked in the life of the people of Orissa?

Ans. The super cyclone in Orissa destroyed many things. It uprooted ancient trees. Houses were swept away. People and animals were killed in large numbers. Lives and families were completely devastated.

Q2. How has Prashant, a teenager, been able to help the people of his village?

Ans. Prashant shows true leadership qualities. He is a determined and calm individual. He motivates people for self help. He indulges them into many tasks like building shelters and arranging food. His presence of mind was of much help at a time of crisis.

Q3. How have the people of the community helped one another? What role do the women of Kalikuda play during these days?

Ans. The people of the community joined hands in a time of utter chaos. Men and youth worked on arranging for food and shelter. While women took care of cooking and looking after orphaned and injured. Women started working in food-for-work programme of different Non-Government Organisation (NGO).

Q4. Why do Prashant and other volunteers resist the plan to set-up institutions for the orphans and widows? What alternatives do they consider?

Ans. Prashant and other volunteers were of the opinion that such institutions were of no help to orphans and widows. Orphans would be devoid of love and affection while the widows would have to live with the stigma of widowhood throughout their lives.

They felt that orphans should be resettled in their own communities, possibly in foster families made up of childless widows and children without adult care.

Q5. Do you think Prashant is a good leader? Do you think young people can get together to help people during natural calamities?

Ans. Prashant is certainly a good leader. He kept his cool in a time of utter chaos. He was the saviour of his community. Like a true leader he showed them the way to fight the crisis. Not only this, he also tried to strengthen his community emotionally by bringing them together.

The Last Leaf

O. Henry

Chapter Sketch

Johnsy and Sue are two friends. One winter Johnsy falls ill. She has no hope and thus thinks her end is near. Sue doesn't agree with her. Johnsy claims that she will die when the last leaf of the ivy creeper falls. Sue asks Mr Behrman for help. The last leaf from the ivy never falls. It was actually painted by Mr Behrman. But the poor old artist dies of pneumonia himself.

Detailed Summary

Johnsy Falls Ill

Sue and Johnsy were two friends who shared a small flat. Johnsy fell seriously ill of pneumonia in November. She would lie in her bed without moving, just gazing out of the window. Sue became very worried. She sent for the doctor. There was no improvement in her condition. The doctor asked Sue if there was anything worrying Johnsy. The doctor told her that Johnsy had made up her mind that she was not going to get well. Medicines wouldn't help her if she has lost all hope.

"When the Last Leaf Falls, I will Die"

Sue tried her best to make Johnsy take an interest in things around her. She talked about clothes and fashions, but Johnsy did not respond. Sue went to her room. Johnsy was whispering something. She was counting the leaves of the ivy outside her window. She told

Sue that she will die when the last leaf of the ivy falls. Sue rubbished her thoughts. Johnsy was so hopeless that she didn't want to have food. She just wanted to look out the window and wait for the last leaf to fall.

Sue goes to Mr Behrman

Sue went to Mr Behrman who lived on the ground floor. He was a painter. Sue shared her worries with him. Even he was amused to learn such a thing and called Johnsy stupid. Sue tried to defend Johnsy. Behrman said that he would give her a visit. Johnsy was sleeping. It was raining very heavily. The leaf would fall any minute. Sue was really very worried. Behrman went back.

Change in Johnsy's Attitude

The next morning, when Johnsy woke up she found the last leaf on the ivy. It was actually green and healthy. Johnsy was sure that the leaf would fall any minute. The leaf did not fall. Johnsy realised that she was a fool. She understood her mistake. The hopelessness had left her. She wanted to live. The doctor also said that he was confident of Johnsy's recovery as she had the will to live. He also informed that Mr Behrman was also suffering from pneumonia but he couldn't be saved.

The Last Leaf

Sue told Johnsy that the janitor found that his clothes and shoes were all wet and he was shivering. He had been out on the stormy night. They found a ladder and lantern also. There were also some brushes and green and yellow colour. He asked Johnsy if she had ever wondered why the last leaf didn't flutter. It was actually Mr Behrman's masterpiece. He painted it in the stormy night.

Exercises

Q1. What was Johnsy's illness? What can cure her, the medicine or the willingness to live?

Ans. Johnsy's may be suffering from pneumonia but her true illness is despondence. She has lost the will to live. No medicine can work for a person in such a case. Only a willingness to live can give enough strength to fight the odds.

Q2. Do you think the feeling of depression Johnsy has is common among teenagers?

Ans. Yes, I believe that the feeling of depression is a common thing among teenagers. Teenagers are not mature enough and hence suffer from emotional defects. When things go wrong, they get panicked easily. Anxiety sets in which leads to emotional imbalance.

Q3. Behrman has a dream. What is it? Does it come true?

Ans. Behrman dreamt of creating a masterpiece. A masterpiece is the creation of an artist which leaves others completely awestruck. He was a painter. Yes, his dream did come true but only after his death.

Q4. What is Behrman's masterpiece? What makes Sue say so?

Ans. The leaf that Mr Behrman drew, was his masterpiece. It was his true talent that the girls could not differentiate it from a real leaf. Sue said so because Behrman had poured his heart out in the painting. Johnsy got motivated only after looking at the 'last leaf'.

8

A House Is Not a Home

Zan Gaudioso

Chapter Sketch

The author moves to high school. He feels lonely and insecure. He misses his old school and friends. One day his house gets burned down and he loses his pet cat. He is deeply hurt. In his time of tragedy, his schoolmates help him out even those who never talked to him. He was overwhelmed. He realised that he was wrong to hold himself back. His house got rebuilt and his cat also got back to him.

Detailed Summary

The Narrator Feels Isolated

The narrator felt awkward at his new school. It felt strange starting over as a freshman. To make matters worse, his closest friends were sent to a different high school. He felt very isolated. He missed his old teachers so much that he would go back and visit them. They encouraged him to enjoy his new surroundings.

Tragedy Strikes

One Sunday afternoon, the narrator was sitting in his house doing his homework. His pet cat was beside him. He had rescued the cat when she was young. Since it was cold, his mother kept stroking the fire. Suddenly, the whole room started to fill with smoke. They rushed out only to find that their house was on fire. His mother ran in and carried out a box full of important documents. Then she again rushed in. The narrator realised that she went for the photographs and letters of his late father. He tried to run behind her but by that time the firemen had arrived and they stopped him.

The Life After

The narrator's pet cat was nowhere to be found. This made him very sad. They went to their grandparent's house to spend the night. His mother made him go to school the next day. He was embarrassed. The changes made him hopeless and everything seemed weird to him. His heart ached for his pet cat. He remembered all the time they had spend together.

A Touching Gesture

The next day at school was even strange. The news of the tragedy had spread. Everybody kept telling him to get ready for the gym. There was a big table set-up with all kinds of stuff on it, just for the narrator. They had taken up a collection and bought him school supplies, notebooks, all kinds of different clothes. It was like Christmas. He was overcome by emotion. People who had never spoken to him before came up to him to introduce themselves. Their genuine outpouring of concern really touched him.

The Narrator's Life got Changed

A month later, he was at the house watching it being rebuilt. But it was different. He wasn't alone. He was with two of his new friends from school. It took a fire for him to stop focusing on his feelings of insecurity and open up to all the wonderful people around me.

Later, his cat was also returned to him. Apparently, she had run away after the fire. But she was found by a woman who searched for her original owners and returned her to them.

Exercises

***Q*1.** What does the author notice one Sunday afternoon? What is his mother's reaction? What does she do?

Ans. While enjoying his Sunday, the author noticed smoke pouring in through the ceiling. They all ran out but his mother tried to recover important documents and his father's photographs. She went in and took these things out.

Q2. Why does he breakdown in tears after the fire?

Ans. The author's home got burned down. Not only this, his pet cat, whom he had brought up since she was a kitten, went missing. He feared that the fire engulfed her. The loss made him cry.

Q3. What is the author deeply embarrassed the next day in school? Which words show his fear and insecurity?

Ans. The narrator's stuff got destroyed in the inferno. His books, homework and other things were all lost. He was not even having decent clothes to wear. His shoes didn't match his clothes. He already felt as an outcast and this made it worse.

The words which show his fear and insecurity are 'weird', 'outcast', 'geek', etc.

Q4. The cat and the author are very fond of each other. How has this been shown in the story? Where was the cat after the fire? Who brings it back and how?

Ans. The cat sleeps in his gowns' pocket; she fiddless with his pen when he is doing his homework. These things give an impression that they were inseparable. The cat escaped the fire and ran far out of fear. A lady found her and from the telephone number written on her caller, tried to find its owner. As the telephone of author's home was dead after the fire so we can assume that the lady must have searched a lot.

Q5. What actions of the schoolmates change the author's understanding of life and people and comfort him emotionally? How does his loneliness vanish and how does he start participating in life?

Ans. Everybody in the new school sympathised with the author's. His schoolmates pooled resources to buy a set of everything he needed in the school. This loving gesture overwhelms the author. Now, the author realises that it was his insecurity which was holding him back. He makes new friends and starts participating in life.

Q6. What is the meaning of "My cat was back and so was I"? Had the author gone anywhere? Why does he say that he is also back?

Ans. After the fire the author feels that he has lost everything. After he gets books and other items from his schoolmates he feels a sense of new found security. Then his cat returns. His statement indicates that he has begun to feel normal again like he used to do in the earlier school.

9

The Accidental Tourist

Bill Bryson

Chapter Sketch

The Accidental Tourist is a humorous account of the absent-mindedness of the narrator. He denies that it's his fault and he can't help it. He keeps getting stuck in awkward situations.

Detailed Summary

The Narrator's Absent-Mindedness

The narrator starts explaining that he is filled with wonder at the amount and diversity of the things people do in their daily lives. He also tells us about how he always ends up making a fool of himself.

The Narrator at the Airport

The narrator was flying with his family. They were checking in Logan Airport in Boston. He remembered that he had inducted himself into British Airways' frequent flyer programme. He was carrying the card in his bag. Unfortunately the zip of his bag got stuck. He tried to release it and in the process he broke it. Everything from his bag started pouring out. All his papers were flying here and there. It was utter chaos for him. He also gashed his finger.

The Narrator Remembers Other Embarrassing Incidents

The narrator was travelling once and he bent down to tie his shoelace. Just then the person sitting in front of him pushed the seat backward. He got pinned to the floor. Once he spilled his drink not on one but on two ladies sitting beside him. Yet another time, when he was talking to a fellow passenger with a pen in his mouth, he didn't realise that the pen had leaked painting his face. This was the reason his wife was always cautious while travelling with him.

The Narrator could not get Free Miles

The narrator always wanted to get free miles. But he couldn't. For some reason or the other he kept missing it. Sometimes due to his mistake or the authorities mistake he couldn't enjoy the privilege. Once as he was about to get a zillion miles of free flying the clerk pointed out that the card was registered on the name of William Bryson and not Bill Bryson thus he missed the opportunity again.

Exercises

Q1. Bill Bryson says, "I am, in short, easily confused." What examples has he given to justify this?

Ans. Bill Bryson is a mess. He forgets the way to the lavatory often. He finds it difficult to remember his hotel room number. He can forget almost everything which is required to carry out our routine activity. He is totally confused and creates a mess of everything he does.

Q2. What happens when the zip on his carry-on bag gives way?

Ans. The contents of his bag come pouring out. They spread all over the place. Moreover, he got his finger hurt. He was bleeding. He could not stand blood which increased his anxiety.

Q3. Why is his finger bleeding? What is his wife's reaction?

Ans. Bill Bryson lashed his finger when he was trying to open his bag and it started bleeding. His wife was not angry. But she was staring at him in wonder. She couldn't believe his luck. How many times do people get their fingers slashed while opening a bag?

Q4. How does Bill Bryson end up in a "crash position" in the aircraft?

Ans. Bill Bryson was travelling. He leaned down to tie his shoelaces. In the meantime the person on the seat ahead of him pushed back his seat. As a result he got stuck in the knelt down position.

Q5. Why are his teeth and gums navy blue?

Ans. Bill Bryson was flying. He was pondering and writing. While pondering over his writing he was chewing on his pen. He started talking to the lady sitting next to him without realising that ink getting into his mouth. As a result his teeth and gums become navy blue.

Q6. Bill Bryson "ached to be suave". Is he successful in his mission? List his 'unsuave' ways.

Ans. Bill Bryson is a mess and thus he ached to be suave. No matter how hard he tried, he always ended up making a fool of himself. He would leave his coat hanging outside the car. He would sit on all kinds of stuff spoiling his clothes. He would also create havoc at every place he went. Be it at dinner or an aeroplane.

Q7. Why do you think Bill Bryson's wife says to the children, "Take the lids off the food for daddy"?

Ans. Bill's wife knew that there was a special talent in Bill Bryson and that was to create a mess of even of the smallest things. In the process he would hurt others also and hence to avoid such a situation his wife asked the children to take the lids off.

Q8. What is the significance of the title?

Ans. The title is quite apt and justified. Bill Bryson was a frequent traveller. But he had a knack for creating accidents. As he is mostly travelling, his worst accidents happen near planes or in them.

10

The Beggar

Anton Chekhov

Chapter Sketch

The story is about a beggar and Sergei, an advocate. The beggar is a vagabond. Sergei tries to put him to the right path. He does this by giving him some work. The beggar works and earns some money. Later, Sergei shifts to another place but before leaving arranges for some work for the beggar. Years later Sergei meets the beggar in a far better condition. The beggar breaks to him that the work was done by Olga and she was the one who changed him.

Detailed Summary

Sergei Meets the Beggar

Sergei encountered a beggar one day. The beggar asked him to have some pity as he hadn't had food for days. Sergei at once recognised him as the beggar whom he met a few days back. Then the beggar had said that he was a student. Sergei caught his lie. The beggar admits the truth.

Sergei Helps the Beggar

Sergei tried to help the beggar by putting him to work. He asked the beggar to chop wood for him. The beggar obliged unwillingly. Olga, Sergei's servant, took the beggar to the shed where he chopped woods. Olga scolded the beggar there. He was not good at work. She called him a drunken spoiled man.

Sergei kept finding different jobs for the beggar. He would clear the snow, beat the dust off old rags, etc.

Sergei Moves to Another Place

Sergei moved to another place. The beggar was certainly not happy that day. Sergei asked him if he could write. The beggar replied in affirmative. Sergei sends him to a friend. Sergei was happy and content as he had put the beggar on the right path.

Two Years Later

One evening Sergei was standing at a ticket window of a theatre. He found the beggar also buying tickets. He asked his name and the beggar replied that his name was Lushkoff. He also said that he earned thirty five roubles a month. This made Sergei happy. He called Lushkoff his godson.

The Change was Brought by Olga

Lushkoff told Sergei that it was Sergei who had helped him but the change was actually brought by Olga the cook. She would scold him and curse him. She cried for him when they were in the shed. Lushkoff was very touched by her concern. Actually it was she who had chopped all the wood for months and Lushkoff hadn't chopped a single time. He was grateful to Olga.

Exercises

Q1. Has Lushkoff become a beggar by circumstances or by choice?

Ans. It appears that harsh circumstances as well as Lushkoff's demeanour are to be blamed for his pitiable condition.

He was a singer in a choir but was thrown out for his drunkenness. He could have found a new job but he resorted to lies and begging.

Q2. What reasons does he give to Sergei for his telling lies?

Ans. Sergei at once realises that Lushkoff was the same beggar who pretended to be a student the other day.

Lushkoff told him that he had to lie because no one will give him anything if he tells the truth.

He couldn't go without lying.

Q3. Is Lushkoff a willing worker? Why, then, does he agree to chop wood for Sergei?

Ans. Lushkoff is certainly not a willing worker. He is a drunkard. He feels ashamed when his lies are caught.

He tries to save his self respect by saying that he can work if he finds it.

He was trapped by his own words and hence consented to work.

Q4. Sergei says, "I am happy that my words have taken effect". Why does he say so? Is he right in saying this?

Ans. Sergei thinks that because of his advice, Lushkoff could get rid of begging.

But actually it was Olga who chopped woods for Lushkoff. It was her tears and care that had brought a change in Lushkoff and not Sergei's kindness.

***Q*5.** Lushkoff is earning thirty five roubles a month. How is he obliged to Sergei for this?

Ans. Lushkoff used to lie and beg for a living. But Sergei was the one who gave him work.

Lushkoff feels that if he hadn't met Sergei then he still would have been a beggar.

He was grateful to Sergei and his cook, Olga.

***Q*6.** During their conversation Lushkoff reveals that Sergei's cook, Olga, is responsible for the positive change in him. How has Olga saved Lushkoff?

Ans. Olga felt pity for Lushkoff. She knew he would not work sincerely. So, she cursed him and shouted at him.

But she had care in her heart. She cried for him and also helped him in his work. Her kindness had an indelible impression on Lushkoff's heart.

It was then that a change came over him and he left his begging ways.

www.ingramcontent.com/pod-product-compliance
Ingram Content Group UK Ltd.
Pitfield, Milton Keynes, MK11 3LW, UK
UKHW021659190726
13853UKWH00001B/356

9 789351 414650